D1572585

Economic Sodomy
How Modern Frauds Work and How To Protect Yourself

by Victor Santoro

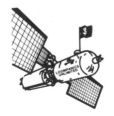

Loompanics Unlimited
Port Townsend, Washington

This book is sold for information purposes only. Neither the author nor the publisher will be held accountable for the use or misuse of the information contained in this book.

Economic Sodomy:
  How Modern Frauds Work and How to Protect Yourself
© 1994 by Victor Santoro

Cover by Jim Blanchard

Published by:
Loompanics Unlimited
PO Box 1197
Port Townsend, WA 98368

Loompanics Unlimited is a division of Loompanics Enterprises, Inc.

ISBN 1-55950-117-0
Library of Congress Catalog Card Number 94-77855

Portions of this book previously appeared in *The Rip-Off Book, Volume 2,* by Victor Santoro, which is currently out of print.

Contents

Introduction

In recent decades, there have been many cultural and technological changes, both to our benefit and to our detriment. Technology can serve positive and negative ends. On one hand, sophisticated security systems, such as laminated photo-ID check guarantee cards are harder to forge, and automatic teller machine personal identification numbers make it impossible for someone who picks up a lost card to use it. On the other, venal and unethical people can always devise methods of circumventing technological security systems, sometimes using even more sophisticated methods, but more often simply playing upon human weaknesses.

In plain language, the bad guys, especially the fraud artists, have refined their techniques and found new ways to take advantage of loopholes in our security systems and the laws dealing with fraud. As we'll see, some of the bad guys even get to make some of the rules.

Recent news about the stealing of funds by top executives of various charities made us aware that even big-name, "legitimate" charities not only have bad eggs within their organizations, but that these are these are often at the top, where they can steal more than low-level employees. We're also more aware of the percentages that professional fund-raising companies charge when they undertake campaigns to raise money for legitimate causes. Many will conduct a telephone campaign for a local orphanage, for example, and keep 80 or 90 percent of the proceeds to cover "operating expenses."

Phony charities have proliferated so much that we regularly see warnings in the media against them. Ann Landers' September 4, 1993 column discusses telephone solicitations and cautions readers to check out any charity they don't know. The column advises anyone who receives a solicitation to find out how much of his contribution will actually go to the charity, and what percentage the fund-raiser pockets.

One of the pitfalls of living in an organized society is having to live by the rules. Sometimes they're inconvenient but necessary, restricting our personal freedom for the sake of not encroaching on that of others. Other rules are useless, or worse, leaving us open to ruthless exploitation by those who know how to manipulate the rules.

Unfortunately, most people still live by obsolete ideas, falsely believing that political and economic doctrines devised a couple of centuries ago still apply in the twentieth century, not realizing that the situation has changed because the entire world has changed. Unfortunately, many doctrines have remained the same.

One obsolete doctrine is that of the "free market." The theory, as taught to high-school economics students, is that various producers make various products for sale on an open market. Customers, exercising their freedom of choice, will buy the best values for the price, and the best manufacturers will thrive. Less efficient or less quality-conscious producers will fail because the people, being intelligent customers, won't buy their products or services.

Traditionally, producer and consumer were roughly equal. Products and services were simple enough for both to understand, and for the consumer to evaluate and make an intelligent choice before buying. Some people, even today, still believe that producer and customer are equal, and that the consumer can defend himself adequately in the marketplace.

Watching a few TV commercials shows how false this idea is today. Advertisers don't sell products on quality or price, but on emotional appeal, suggesting that drinking a certain beer, or buying a certain car, will result in being surrounded by attractive women. The fallacy of the consumer's informed judgment is clearest in serious fields, such as buying medical care, and trivial ones, such as buying a home computer. To be properly informed, the consumer must have a fairly good working knowledge of each field, and usually he doesn't. This leaves him vulnerable to abuses.

In the life-and-death field of medicine, consumers often don't understand the issues well because doctors conspire to keep them ignorant. There's no such conspiracy among computer manufacturers, but the subject is extremely complex, and a higher education is necessary to understand it fully.

Ignorance isn't critical when buying a $2,000 computer. A "lemon" can be annoying, and the buyer may demand a refund, but personal danger is slight. It's much more serious when buying medical care. The consumer who receives unnecessary treatment or surgery is lucky not to have his health impaired, and is vulnerable to side-effects and possibly crippling complications. Sometimes he dies.

"Consumer fraud" is a twentieth century term. While sharp hawkers of high-priced and inferior goods have always existed, deceiving the public was never as systematized as it is today. Modern "robber barons" steal more money legally than their ancestors ever did, and in a more systematic manner. At the same time, many of the old scams are still with us, although in modern guises. Con artists are very creative, constantly devising new ways to fool people.

Today we can divide scams into two categories:

1. Individual scams, in which individual, unorganized con artists prey upon unwary individuals.
2. Institutional scams, protected by law, practiced by members of politically powerful occupational groups such as doctors, lawyers, and advertisers. An example is mandatory auto insurance, where the consumer is forced to pay for an insurance policy to operate a motor vehicle. This produces a captive clientele, forced to pay

Economic Sodomy

4

whatever rates the insurance companies establish. This is the modern-day version of the "protection" racket.

If you operate a motor vehicle in such a situation, you have no choice. If you try to operate your vehicle without insurance, you'll pay a penalty. Institutional scams leave the ordinary citizen naked and defenseless, because the power of the government sustains the fraud artists.

Today, these aren't pure categories. They tend to overlap because fraud artists are as ingenious as honest members of society, and strive constantly to find new variations of their scams to circumvent the law. In this book, we'll cover the various categories and those in between, examining some very closely. This will give you an idea of how they work, and suggest ways of protecting yourself against some of them.

Make no mistake about it: you won't be able to avoid them all. There are too many, and you can't be both vigilant and strong everywhere at once. However, you'll be able to keep your head above water at a time when most people can't.

More importantly, this book will show you how to fight back, using both passive and active means of defense and counter-attack. This is the most important point of all. While many people bow their heads and give up, feeling that "the system" is too powerful to fight, you'll be able to fight back effectively, at least part of the time. The twentieth century has brought with it not only more scams and frauds, but more ways for the victims to strike back effectively.

This book discusses various categories of fraud, and each topic contains a section on how to protect yourself. Frankly, most defenses against being ripped off are just common sense, requiring only a cautious attitude and close examination of anything that seems too good to be true. The last part, "Defense and Counter-Attack," discusses advanced techniques you can use to make life harder for people trying to rip you off.

Although political correctness mandates using non-"sexist" language, we'll ignore this to avoid awkward phrasing such as "he/she" and "him and her." The fact is that fraud artists, like other criminals, are still predominantly male, and it's both factually and grammatically better to refer to them as "he."

How Frauds Work

To understand fraud artists and how they rip you off, you have to know their basic techniques. Understanding helps you build defenses against them.

Frauds depend on taking advantage of human nature, because con artists are masters of practical psychology and experts at using your good nature, respect for authority, and charitable feelings to separate you from your money. If you're greedy, con men will take advantage of this weakness, as well.

Con artists love to say that "you can't cheat an honest man." This sentiment is as big a con as any of the games they play on you, because it implies that if you let yourself be defrauded, it's merely because you're as dishonest as the criminal who defrauded you, but not as smart. The implication that you live in the same moral sewer as he does justifies the fraud artist in his own mind, because it reinforces his belief that any dishonest tactic is legitimate because "it's a jungle out there."

Let's study the basic tactical principles fraud artists use against you.

Charity

When you give to charity, you're not doing it for material gain, but from an altruistic wish to help others. You get a warm feeling inside, and con artists will help you attain this warm feeling, for a price.

Credulity

Most of us assume that what someone else tells us is true, unless it's so patently false as to be ridiculous. This is because we've been brought up to be truthful, and we tend to believe that most other people think the way we do. Bad Mistake! Con men take advantage of our good nature to fool us, because they are skillful liars.

Urgency

A fraud is usually a "limited time" offer, and the con man urges us to act now, before the opportunity vanishes. The fraud artist creates the sense of urgency through various stratagems, so that his victims don't have time to think carefully about the deal, and certainly no time to check it out with the Better Business Bureau or the police.

Authority

Many fraud artists use the power of authority to compel people to do what they want them to do. A doctor who advises his patient to submit to unnecessary treatments is using the power of his authority to line his pockets at the patient's expense. Some fraud artists use the power of the law to recruit victims, as in the case of mandatory auto insurance.

Greed

Finally, some people want something for nothing, despite the common-sense observation that "there's no such thing as a free lunch." Enough said.

Now that we've gotten the basics under our belts, let's take a close look at the many ways people become victims of fraud.

Part One:
Little Cons

While big-time operators soar in the stratosphere of megabuck business frauds, down in the lower regions smaller enterprisers are getting their share. Unfortunately, these small-time fraud artists tend not to pick on the bigger and wealthier people who can defend themselves, but on those who can least afford to lose their assets.

Chapter 1
Employee Theft

Rightly or wrongly, businessmen and business organizations claim that employee theft costs them more each year than shoplifting, armed robberies, burglaries, and other "outside" crimes.[1] This is easy to believe, with the qualification that the "employees" involved may be as high-ranking as corporate presidents.

There's a widespread and self-serving belief among businessmen that only the lower classes can be dishonest. This fits in with businessmen's perceptions of themselves as a superior breed, vital enterprisers above and apart from the rest of plodding, witless humanity.

One authority on employee theft, echoing the beliefs prominent in the field, advises strongly that an employer check every job applicant's references before hiring.[2]

Alexander, a former retailer, points out that any applicant, no matter how qualified he seems, may be dishonest. He states that many applicants falsify their qualifications and employment records. With this dishonest beginning, employees go on to rob their employers blind.

This authority provides an impressive catalog of the many ways in which employees can appropriate company property and funds. Switching price tags, handing wrapped packages to confederates, and not ringing up sales are three of the many tricks dishonest retail employees use. A United Press article, dated December 6, 1965, confirms this. Allegedly, dishonest employees pilfer 43 percent of the stock shrinkage, while shoplifters account for only 30 percent.

Conventional wisdom is to trust nobody, with the main burden of suspicion falling on recent hires and lower-level employees. Old and trusted employees are never above suspicion, and it's wise to be very watchful.[3] One "tip" for spotting thieves and embezzlers is to scrutinize very carefully the long-term and apparently hard-working employee who never takes a vacation.

Many employers, concerned with the prospect of dishonesty among their staffs, focus their attention on low-level employees, and often this surveillance includes asking very personal questions of employees in a show of fake friendliness and personal interest. Employers, who would resent such probing questions if asked of themselves, are quite aggressive in prying into subordinates' personal lives.

Countermeasures taken by employers include undercover agents to ferret out evidence of theft.[4] Most undercover agents, however, are placed in the "back shop," not the executive suite. We see this class distinction in many businesses, where security guards at the employee's gate examine packages carried by low-level employees, not top executives. An executive can make off with a box of paperclips or a calculator for his children just as easily as a low-paid shop employee. An executive may see taking materials home from the office as a fringe benefit of his position. He also has access to items of much higher value.

An executive, trusted by his employer, has a virtual license to steal. He can be looting accounts, selling proprietary information to a competitor, accepting bribes, and participating in a variety of rip-offs.

Techniques of theft are almost infinite. Each industry has its own assortment of techniques, and some even have developed a folklore of theft. Some methods are mainly for the lower-level employees, while others are the province of upper management. Yet others belong to both, because they're accessible to both. Let's examine a few.

Looting fiduciary accounts is profitable and almost undetectable. The most successful way of doing this is to use the assets as short-term, interest-free loans. Let's say that an employee, whether a simple clerk in a bank or brokerage house or a top-level executive, wants to play the market. If he digs into an account's assets and "borrows" negotiables, uses them for a successful transaction and then replaces them, he's got no problem. His short-term looting will remain undetected. It becomes unraveled only if the deal goes sour, and the "borrower" loses more than he can replace. If the looting's taken place with a fairly inactive account, it may be some time before anyone discovers the shortage.

Part of the reason such scams work so well is that people have been conditioned to accept pieces of paper as having value. This isn't restricted only to paper currency, where there are many abuses, most by the government. Conservative economists lament the flood of paper currency, pointing out that without precious metal backing it, printing paper money leads to inflation.

Unfortunately, people also accept other kinds of paper as a matter of course. Stocks and bonds are negotiable. So is a warehouse receipt from a bonded warehouse. On a lower level, a "gift certificate" has cash value at the store issuing it. All of these have cash values, but are without the protection of the Federal Deposit Insurance Corporation and other government agencies which guarantee the value of currency. They're also not printed on high-security paper with restricted distribution. This makes them easy to duplicate, counterfeit, and even create from scratch, using a fictitious financial institution. This creates many opportunities for dishonesty.

How does this work? It's easy.

Let's say you have a counterfeit thousand-dollar bill. You can try to pass it, but you'll encounter problems. You can't use it at a supermarket or gas station. Even if the clerk accepted it as genuine, making change for a thousand-dollar bill would be difficult. You'd have to go to a bank, where a teller and perhaps the manager would scrutinize the bill with great care. You might have to show I.D. and bank employees might even record your name and address.

On the other hand, if you're a purchasing agent or other executive with line authority in a solvent and respectable firm, you can issue purchase orders to a dummy company that has practically nothing in assets, consisting only of a post office box and printed stationery. The responsible executive of the dummy company (it can be you, using an alias) signs the purchase order's acknowledgment copy. A four-part billing form is the next step. One copy serves as the shipping record or packing slip. Another is the invoice. You staple the packing slip to the purchase order, and send the invoice copy to your accounting department.

Paperwork routing varies with the company, but usually the accounting department employees will "vouch" the invoice with a "receiving record." This is an internally-generated slip verifying that the material was received and counted by a company employee. In practice, these are easy to fake. It's necessary only to walk out to the receiving department and write one. The forms are serially-numbered, but this means nothing except as a way to locate a particular shipment. The serial numbers don't provide proof of authenticity.

A slightly simpler way to work this scam is to have the "shipment" go to a remote site, where no receiving record is kept. You simply "sign it off" at the appropriate time, and accounting cuts a check to your dummy company.

Another way is to have your dummy company bill the real firm for services, not products. A "trucking company" works well for this purpose. One person who tried this was a lowly clerk, and his employer exposed him after noticing his opulent lifestyle. The employer couldn't reconcile this high living with the stingy salary he was paying him.[5]

The types of theft committed by the executive are varied, imaginative, and usually more rewarding than the simple pilferage of the low-level nine-to-fiver. Part of the reason is that the line between legitimate perquisites (perks) and outright fraud is very blurred. Many acts that would get a low-level employee fired are acceptable for an executive. Let's look at a few:

The "expense account," also known as a "cheat sheet," is simply a way of padding one's income. Executives routinely charge "business lunches" to the company. Line workers, even if they discuss their jobs over lunch, are never allowed to charge them to their employer's bill.

It's important here to make the distinction between the Internal Revenue Code and company practice. Although new provisions in the law have disallowed flagrantly abusive deductions, this merely means that the company can no longer deduct them on its tax return. It doesn't prohibit companies from reimbursing executives for them.

The "take-home car" is one popular fringe benefit that has traditionally been the executive's. Changes in the Internal Revenue Code now require an executive with a take-home car to report his commuting mileage as income, but it's still a free ride for him. Paying mileage only means that he gets a rental car at nominal rates.

By contrast, the blue-collar employee must buy his own car, pay for the plates and insurance, and keep it greased, oiled, and repaired. He can't deduct a penny of this.

Company credit cards provide another area for abuse. In principle, they allow the fast-moving executive the freedom to pay for transportation, lodging, and entertainment, to carry on the company's business. In real life, we know the actual purpose: to provide supplementary and non-taxable income for the top brass. The executive can use his credit card to put gas into his personal vehicle, although theoretically it's reserved for the company car.

The way this system works is that the executive is advised at the outset how much he's allowed to run up in expenses per year. Within this limit, he can spend pretty much as he wishes. His employer will not send an investigator to determine if the woman with whom he shared a hotel room during a business trip was really his wife. The accounting department will not ask him if the restaurant receipt marked "Dinner with J. Smith" was truly a business meeting.

Another form of supplementary income is the company-owned and maintained resort. The largest corporations maintain private hotels, game preserves, and even private islands to entertain clients and business associates. These facilities are also for holding "conferences" and "seminars" of various sorts. The amount of business discussed during these sessions is not in proportion to the expenses involved.

Bribery is a form of theft, and some executives accept bribes. A purchasing agent who awards contracts in return for a consideration harms his company. The bribe may be a low-interest "loan" that need not be repaid. The "kick-back" isn't necessarily in cash. It can be a stock option, privately offered to certain deserving individuals. It can be a consideration to a relative. It can take the form of being a "guest" of the vendor on a vacation trip. There are so many ways of arranging pay-offs today that it's virtually impossible to trace them all.

Sometimes, the bribery is self-bribery, as with a conflict of interest. One instructive hypothetical case is that of Malicious Manufacturing.

Mr. Stiff, Executive Director of Malicious Manufacturing, was also a major stockholder in the Royal Screw and Bolt Corporation. The Chief of Purchasing at Malicious Manufacturing was compelled to place most of the orders for fasteners with Royal Screw, at Mr. Stiff's order. In the trade, this is known as a "directed source." Royal Screw was often late in deliveries, harming the company's projects, but Mr. Stiff continued to earn money on each contract both ways, because he had a finger in each pie.[6]

Ever wonder why so many retired generals and admirals get high-level jobs with defense contractors when they leave the service? This is a simple, yet very workable form of bribery: the delayed pay-off. It continues to work despite a law forbidding military officers to accept employment with businesses dealing with the Department of Defense upon retirement.

Let's look at another hypothetical case:

The General Specialty Corporation, a major defense contractor, is seeking to sell a new jet fighter to the U.S. Navy. On the staff of one of their subsidiaries, the General Washing Machine Company, is Retired Admiral Smedley Sturdley. He's valuable partly because he knows his way around Pentagon procurement circles, and partly because his cushy slot inspires other naval officers in the procurement division. His record speaks for itself.

During his years of active service, the admiral was a proponent of the General XF-1, a naval jet fighter that was over-publicized but under-powered. Known among the lower ranks as the "flying coffin," it was inadequate against any major power's naval jets, although an

XF-1 did shoot down an aircraft of the Arabian Air Force. Despite the XF-1's failure in naval service, it proved to be a great financial success for General Specialty and for Admiral Sturdley. Upon retirement, the admiral was able to supplement his generous government pension with a $200,000 per year job with General Specialty's subsidiary.

Now, General Specialty is promoting its new XF-2, allegedly the latest thing in aerial warfare and equipped with guns, rockets, and frequency-agile air-intercept radar. Despite this impressive array of hardware, it's already known as the "kamikaze" among Navy test pilots because of landing gear that collapses when needed most. It's also overweight and overpriced, and the new Russian KK-35 can run rings around it at half the cost. Admiral Hardnose, Sturdley's successor, has grumbled about the XF-2, hinting darkly that he'll recommend purchase of the Foxworth Ferret instead.

Sturdley goes to work. He arranges to have dinner with Hardnose one evening. The conversation was private, but the next day Admiral Hardnose came out in favor of the XF-2.

This is the way the system works. In one sense, it's terribly wasteful of taxpayers' dollars, which buy expensive junk. In another sense, the system tends to assure peace, for two reasons:

1. These expensive toys won't perform as needed, and no matter how hard the government huffs and puffs, it won't go to war except against third-rate powers such as Saddam Hussein's Iraq, and then only with plenty of allies.
2. The purpose of heavy armaments is not to support a war, but to earn large profits for their manufacturers.

Thus, we see that "employee theft" covers a wide field, from the nickel-and-dime stealing by low-paid employees to high-level wheeling and dealing by powerful executives. Although low-level employees receive the most publicity when caught, in dollar volume they can't begin to match the big characters because they don't have access to much. The clerk slips a box of paperclips into his pocket, while the vice-president hijacks the company.

Notes:

1. *Stealing*, Alfred Alexander and Val Moolman, NY, Cornerstone Library, 1969, p. 10. Although this is an old text, recent estimates repeat the statement that insiders steal much more than outsiders.
2. *Stealing*, p. 54. This is good advice, ignored by many employers trying to save a buck. Checking references takes time, effort, and money, and many employers try to save by using pencil-and-paper "honesty" tests provided by psychological charlatans. See also "How to Avoid Hiring Mistakes," *Jewelers Circular Keystone*, July 15, 1990, v161, p. 346. There is no substitute for careful background checking.
3. *Stealing*, pp. 58-59.
4. *Ibid.*, p. 63. Also see "Going Undercover: An Inside or an Outside Job?," Article by Mark B. Rosen, *Security Management*, June, 1992, pp. 52-53.
5. *Ibid.*, p. 17.
6. Personal associates of the author.

Chapter 2
Fake Cops

The official police in America have had their corruption scandals. One reason is that there are hordes of quasi- and semi-official "police officers," such as security guards, reserve officers, sheriffs' posse members, and other card-carrying amateur law enforcement agents. The United States has seen, however, the effects of its fragmented law enforcement in parallel police, tangential police, and outright fake police agents.

One aggressive pseudo-police officer was George Adams, who harassed saloon owners at the turn of the century in New York City.[1] He'd flash a badge and claim to be a member of a vigilance committee or a plainclothesman, and extort money from his victims. Adams got carried away, though, because he then began bull-dogging real cops. He flashed a captain's badge in a police station and shouted orders, but a sergeant phoned headquarters to verify his identity. He didn't check out, and the indignant and vengeful officers inflicted severities on him.

Local law enforcement officials sometimes aggrandize their powers and try to pass themselves off as more than they are. One New

Jersey Justice of the Peace claimed to be in the "Federal Secret Service," and he ran a business on the side selling documents and badges to anyone who paid him $100 for the privilege of becoming a "special agent."[2]

County sheriffs in this country are elected officials, and often hand out badges to campaign supporters. With the popularity of the "cop culture" on television and in films, a certain proportion of our citizens have become "badge-happy." Others are more practical, knowing that flashing a badge at a traffic cop will often avert a citation.

Until recently, this handing out of police credentials was common. Many, many rural and small-town citizens were "special deputies" and "posse members." Almost all states have passed laws requiring police officers to be "certified," which means that they must have had a specified amount of training and met established standards to obtain certification. This precludes creating instant deputies, but ways around the system still exist, and this results in our parallel police and tangential police.

Police agencies tend to regard themselves as short-staffed, and many try to recruit "reservists," unpaid volunteers who take a limited amount of training to attain a reserve certification. This authorizes them to carry firearms and badges. Some states have several levels of reserve training and certification. The lower level allows the reservist to be "second man," which means working only under the direction of a fully-certified officer. The next level is "car commander," which for all practical purposes means a fully-trained, fully-certified police officer.

In many jurisdictions, reservists and posse members form social clubs, rather than adjuncts to professional police organizations. Those who pass the relatively lax qualifications spend minimal time supplementing the police they serve, but a lot of time in social functions. Some "posse meetings" are merely drinking sessions, and the membership list includes the community's upper crust.

While there are extremely capable and dedicated reservists and possemen, most are not "real cops" but only pretenders. They're assigned to light duties while the regular force performs the real work.

One deception occurs when some professional writers seek to parlay their reserve status into credentials for writing authoritatively on police topics. A good number of police officers who read law enforcement magazines are more receptive to articles by those they see as fellow officers than those by civilians.

Certain police magazines have published articles by authors posing in uniform to give the reader the impression that they're actual full-time working cops when they're merely part-timers. One recent book on police firearms has a photograph of its author on the back flap, standing in uniform beside a patrol car. This man was a reservist at the time he wrote that book.

Another reservist is simply "badge-happy." A high school teacher by occupation, he has never served as a full-time police officer, but he attends as many police conventions as possible, passing himself off as a detective sergeant.[3] He spends his summer vacations visiting police agencies in other countries, and generally lives and breathes police work.

Some pseudo-cops, however, are dangerous. One notable figure was Gaston B. Means, who had a long, almost unbelievable career in "law enforcement." Means, after working at other occupations, found work with the Burns Detective Agency in 1910. He gained experience with this agency until he found a lucrative sucker, a rich widow. He convinced her that her estate needed "managing," and persuaded her to accept him as a combination protector and investment counselor.

During the several years of their relationship, she turned over about $150,000 to him, which he kept for his own use. By 1917, she may have started to become suspicious, because she asked him for an accounting. He invited her to go for a walk in the woods with him, then reported her as the victim of an "accidental" gunshot wound. The body had a bullet in the back of the head behind the left ear. The rural coroner's jury handed down a verdict of accidental homicide.[4] This chain of strange events concluded with a murder trial, in which the jury found the death to be suicide.

When the United States entered World War I, Means found another lucrative line — selling his services as an "intelligence agent" to the British, the Germans, and the U.S. Army Intelligence Service. Means' efforts in this area shows how intelligence services, desperate for information, allow themselves to be victimized by fakers and people working both sides of the street. Many intelligence officers are not "intelligent" at all, but are simply dolts who buy bogus information from tricksters.

After the armistice, Means found a job in the Justice Department's Bureau of Investigation, the antecedent of today's FBI. At the time, just before the start of the J. Edgar Hoover Era, the Bureau was corrupt, staffed by political appointees, not professional law enforcement officers. Means was merely one of many who collected government paychecks for inept work.[5]

Means' career was extraordinary, not because the man was a genius, but because he was surrounded by idiots. His discovery of the extra-marital affair between President Harding and Nan Britton was due to their foolishness and indiscretion, not his investigative genius.

After the Harding Affair he earned his keep by offering "protection" to wealthy people against anarchists, communists, and other threatening figures. He stimulated his business by sending threats himself.

It was the Lindbergh kidnapping, however, that showed Means in the worst light. Although the Lindbergh Case had attracted swarms of official police officers, they were unable to find the child or his kidnapper.[6]

A foolish woman, also wealthy, sought out Means and engaged his services to find the missing child. Evlyn Walsh McLean, with more money than brains, believed Means' claim that he could find the child using his underworld contacts. He asked her for $100,000 as ransom payment, and another $4,000 for his "expenses." He never recovered the child, nor did he give back the money. This flim-flam finally resulted in a prison sentence and Means died behind bars.

Thus we see that there's a small subculture of cop freaks, wanna-bes, and con men who get good mileage from impersonating law enforcement officers. Some do it for ego. Others, such as writers who pass themselves off as bona fide police officers, gain marginal benefits by enhancing their credibility. Finally, some are hard-core con artists, like Gaston Means and the many lesser figures who impersonate officers in the "badger game."

Notes:

1. *Hustlers & Con Men*, Jay Robert Nash, NY, M. Evans & Company, 1976, p. 279.
2. *Ibid.*, p. 279.
3. Personal acquaintance of the author.
4. *Hustlers & Con Men*, p. 289.
5. Whatever J. Edgar Hoover's faults were, and he had many, tolerating corruption among subordinates was not one of them. He uprooted incompetent and corrupt agents with the zealotry of a religious fanatic. The irony of his fifty-year reign was that Hoover was sexually kinky himself, and corrupt in a larger sense, because he made more effort to glorify himself and his organization than he did to carry out his official duties.
6. Among the police officers involved was H. Norman Schwartzkopf, Sr., Superintendent of the New Jersey State Police and father of the General Schwartzkopf of Desert Storm fame.

Chapter 3
Fraudulent Patients

There have been accounts of people obtaining medical and surgical care for imaginary conditions. This is called "polysurgery,"[1] as well as other terms, and usually isn't a fraud in the legal sense because the patient pays for services rendered. The deception consists of the patient fooling himself and the surgeon into thinking he needs surgery. Evidently, this is mainly a mental-health problem, not a police problem. However, some patients set out to deceive for monetary or other gains, including obtaining prescription narcotics.

In recent years, doctors and pharmacists have seen many instances of drug addicts obtaining prescription drugs by deception. Stealing prescription pads and forging a doctor's signature is a common tactic. Obtaining a legitimate prescription from a doctor is another. The usual way to do this is to claim pain in an area where it's hard for the doctor to disprove the claim. A "backache" can arise from causes that don't show up on an X-ray. So can neck pains of various types, including the "whiplash" known to doctors and personal injury lawyers.

Doctors faced with such cases have reason to be cautious, but have little hope of disproving the deception. The fraudulent patient's pattern is to seek out a strange doctor. If the physician asks why the patient isn't seeing his regular or family doctor, there's always a ready explanation. One common reason is that the patient is newly arrived in town, with his family doctor hundreds or thousands of miles away. If the physician remains suspicious and wants to check it out, a phone call may establish that the patient is lying, either because he's not a patient of the physician he names, or because he's suffered no injury as claimed. A canny "patient" can always have another strategem ready, though, giving the doctor the number of a public telephone in a remote area to call. Upon failing to get through, the physician may give the "patient" the benefit of the doubt and write him a prescription for a pain-killer anyway.

The Scottsdale Faker

Recently, one "patient" who went all the way came to light. This man not only solicited treatments and prescriptions, but used fake insurance claims to pay for them. This happened in Scottsdale, Arizona, and consisted of a series of systematic and consistent ruses.[2]

He never went to the same physician more than once, and used as many as nine aliases. His method of operation was to appear at a doctor's office or hospital emergency room and claim to have hurt his back on the job. He usually named an out-of-state construction company as his employer, to delay inquiries.

Filling his prescriptions worked the same way. He victimized a local chain of pharmacies repeatedly, possibly because their system of obtaining payment was compatible with his scam.

Providing the name of the insurer for payment followed the same pattern. The man would give the name of an out-of-state employer or insurance company, and eventually the claim would disclose that no such employee existed. In other instances, the company he named did not exist. In workmen's compensation claims, the state agency had no record of the individual, account, or the employer.

In one instance, this faker "fainted" in a restaurant, and was brought to the emergency room. He was there interviewed by police and a photograph was taken. The name he provided was fake, but this did not come to light until several days afterward. Police have speculated that the subject is a "drifter."

This man has apparently defrauded numerous doctors and hospitals in the area, not only in the City of Scottsdale. The reason he's been so successful is that he's bold, and doctors and hospitals feel intimidated by people claiming treatment for injuries because in this area, there have been recent scandals of seriously ill or injured people being turned away by private hospitals because they could not furnish proof of ability to pay. The practice of "dumping" critically ill patients onto the county hospital has received enough media attention to make doctors and hospitals cautious about turning away patients. The prospect of a lawsuit is also important.

Claiming a back injury is a safe bet, because strained muscles and ligaments are already known to be extremely painful and don't show up on X-rays. Hospital personnel also know that many ill or injured people show up without medical insurance cards, especially if there's been an accident. This opens the door for a slick talker fraudulently to obtain both treatment and drugs.

The outlook for recovery of money if the man is ever apprehended is bleak. If he's truly a drifter, he typically owns nothing but his clothes.

The Larger Picture

Recently, the National Health Care Anti-Fraud Association reported that medical fraud may account for up to $75 billion annually in this country. Medical-injury frauds can result in workmen's compensation claims, while auto-injury fraud hits conventional insurance companies.[3]

Two common types of fraudulent claims are soft-tissue injuries, which do not show up on X-rays, and stress-related disabilities, which are intangible and very hard to evaluate. Another kind is the faked motor vehicle accident scam, aimed at defrauding insurance companies. The scammers prepare an injury car, with several occupants to multiply the value of the eventual claims, and stage an accident by stopping abruptly in front of a lumbering commercial vehicle. The rear-end collision places the commercial vehicle at fault, laying the way for injury claims against the company. Some vehicle-accident scammers, known as "cappers" in their lingo, go as far as to have another vehicle box-in the commercial vehicle to prevent it from avoiding collision by changing lanes.

Medical fraud by phony patients, overall, is far less than the frauds committed by doctors and hospitals against their patients, though. Doctors take advantage of the weakened and vulnerable state of their patients, while patient fraud artists are going up against some of the smartest people in town, as well as the investigatory organizations employed by insurance companies.

Notes:

1. *Man Against Himself*, Karl Menninger, NY, Harcourt, Brace & Company, 1938, pp. 259-278.
2. *Arizona Republic*, January 17, 1986.
3. *Security Management*, November, 1993, pp. 31-35.

Chapter 4
Miscellaneous "Short Cons"
And Other Frauds

As society becomes more complex, it provides more windows of opportunity for fraud artists. Frauds become more refined, but not necessarily more complex. The term, "short con," refers to the quick scheme, involving little preparation and a quick pay-off. This is in contrast to the elaborate and time-consuming frauds, such as the Ponzi Scheme, that take weeks or months to execute.

The twentieth century has made possible scams that were inconceivable in earlier years. Examples of high-tech scams we'll discuss are credit card and ATM scams, cellular phone frauds, and fraudulent electronic tax filing, among others.

Not all frauds are aimed at taking money directly from you. Some are just schemes to take or borrow something you have for the fraud artist's benefit.

Taking Over Your Identity

Methods of "paper tripping" have proliferated since the publication of Frederick Forsyth's *Day of the Jackal* and various how-to manuals that have appeared in its wake. Yet, new methods seem to spring up almost daily. One practiced con man on the lam devised a quick way to steal other people's identities for short-term covers. His purpose was not to live under the other person's I.D. for any length of time, but simply to travel under the cover, to evade the authorities.

He placed an ad in a small Southern California newspaper, wording the ad to attract people who were down on their luck and credit rating. The phone number he gave was that of his motel, and he took "job applications" from about fifty people until he checked out the following day. He recorded their birth dates and places of birth, social security numbers, credit histories, and other personal information that would enable him to find people who matched him in age, sex, and physical characteristics. With date and place of birth, he was able to send away for their birth certificates, the first step towards building a new identity.

Once he had obtained birth certificates, he was able to obtain genuine driver's licenses and other official and semi-official paperwork to support the aliases. He then went to Colorado, and using one alias, Jerry Anthony Greene, obtained a Colorado driver's license.[1] After that, he moved on, finally leaving the country and escaping to Europe under another alias.

Protecting Yourself

Ultimately, you cannot prevent someone from sending for your birth certificate without your knowledge and constructing a past for himself based on your identity. However, you can avoid making it easy for him. Don't give out personal information, such as your date and place of birth, to people who call you. Be positively stingy about personal details you give out, even to acquaintances.

"Rapid Tax Refunds"

Electronic income tax refund filing saves time, no doubt, and it speeds up obtaining a refund, if you're entitled to it, from the IRS. However, some tax preparers who include electronic filing among their services offer their clients "instant" tax refunds, for a fee, of course. The average fee is $50, and for an average-size refund of $978, this comes to an annual percentage rate of 88.6 percent.[2] This isn't actually fraud, because there's no deception involved, but it's a sucker trap for the unwary. However, some have exploited electronic filing for their own purposes, as we'll see later in this chapter.

Various Car Buyer Con Games

If you're putting your vehicle up for sale privately, watch out for this fraud. A person purporting to be interested in your car telephones you to make an appointment to see the car, and leaves his address and phone number with you. He tells you to call him at work, which is at a major company in your area. You verify the number in the directory, and it turns out to be genuine. So far, everything appears above-board.

That evening or the next day, the "buyer" appears, praises your vehicle, and asks if he may drive it for a few days just to be sure he likes it. He offers you a "down payment" of a couple of hundred dollars to gain your confidence in his sincerity. You hand him the keys, and he drives off.

When he's due to return the car or buy it, he doesn't show. You phone him, and he gives you an excuse for not having returned it. He also says he thinks your asking price is too high, and offers you much less than what you think it's worth. Worried, you demand the car back. You go to his place of business to pick up your car, and have no trouble getting it back. Of course, you do not refund his earnest money, as he apparently has reneged on the sale after driving your car for a week.

As you drive away, you notice that, although you'd provided him with a full tank for his test drive, the tank is almost empty, and if you'd bothered to note the odometer reading at the outset, you see that he's driven several hundred miles in your vehicle. You regret not having sold the car, but congratulate yourself on having retrieved your car intact.

What's wrong with this picture? Have you seen what it costs to rent a car these days? This fellow has just gotten the use of your car for two hundred dollars, much less than what he would have had to pay a rental agency. He's also used your gas.

Protecting Yourself

Never let anyone have your vehicle for more than a short test drive, unless it's someone you know very well, such as a neighbor or relative. If a buyer insists upon driving your car for a week, politely but firmly suggest that he rent a similar model from a car rental agency.

The Chop Shop Game

Another con game is to get the keys to your car for a quick drive around the block. If you let the "buyer" go off alone, that's the last you'll see of your car. Before you can report it to the police, your car will be in a "chop shop" being dismantled for parts, and you'll never see the "buyer" again.

Another aspect of protecting yourself is to be aware of the demand for parts from your car on the black market. If you have a late model, especially a flashy Camaro or similar vehicle, you run a much greater risk of having it stolen by stealth or deception than if you own an older model. The reasons are that there are more older models in junk yards waiting to be stripped for parts, and that newer model parts bring much more money because of their scarcity. If you can be satisfied driving a five-year old Volvo, which is a solid and substantial car despite its dowdy appearance, you run far less risk of having it stolen.

Protecting Yourself

The countermeasure to this type of fraud is obvious. Never let a stranger drive off alone with your car, even if he shows you his driver's license. If he's intent on stealing your car, any driver's license he shows you will be stolen or forged. If he's legitimate, he won't object to your accompanying him.

Over The Border

If you live in a state that borders on Mexico, beware the over-the-border scam. A purported buyer drives away with your vehicle, straight for the border. By the time you decide to report your vehicle stolen, it's probably already in Mexico, where the thief can get several times its U.S. value. Don't be reassured by the recent tightening of Mexican auto sale restrictions. Forged papers will allow a thief to slip your vehicle over the border and resell it on the other side.

Spare Parts

This doesn't result in the loss of your car, but only a quick scavenging for spare parts. This game works for someone who owns the same model car you do, and who wants to get some replacement parts for nothing. The "buyer" shows up and asks for a test drive. If you let him go off by himself, he'll drive your car to where he can remove the battery, tires, or whatever else he may need. He replaces your new tires or battery with his worn-out ones, and returns the car to you. Of course, he doesn't buy it.

Stripping and replacing the components may take some time, much longer than the few minutes' test drive you'd anticipated. The "buyer" is counting on your being so relieved to see your car again that you won't scrutinize it carefully for substitutions.

Protecting Yourself

The counter-measure is simple: never let someone you don't know take you car out of your sight. Go with any prospective buyer for several reasons. The most obvious is to ensure that he returns your vehicle. Another is to observe what he does with it. A prospective buyer who gets into a minor accident may not report it to the seller, but simply return the car, hoping you won't notice a dent in a fender or bumper. Later, if you ask him about the damage, he'll simply state that the car was that way when you handed him the keys.

Selling "Bargain" Cars

A scam recently came to light in the Miami, Florida, area which involved selling cars stolen from rental agencies. The "seller" was well-dressed, and flashed a gold badge to impress prospective buyers when he told them that the vehicles had been confiscated by Dade County, which was now letting the vehicles go at bargain prices. Low as the prices were ($1,850 for a late-model car, for example) the con man did not demand the entire purchase price at once, but only a $1,000 deposit, for which he handed the buyer the car keys to let him drive it until the deal went through. People who sought him to pay the balance and receive the paperwork found that the "seller" had disappeared.[3]

The Tenant Fraud

A tenant wanting to raise a few hundred dollars quickly puts his rented house up for sale or rent. When you arrive, he poses as the owner, and gladly shows you the house. If you decide to rent or buy it, he accepts your deposit, but when it comes time for you to move in or close the sale, he's disappeared with your money.

Protecting Yourself

Never give a deposit to anyone purporting to be the "owner" of the property. Always work through a title or escrow company, and make sure that you make your check out to the title company, not the person claiming to be the owner.

Apartment Rental Woes

In some locales, such as Mesa, Arizona, Portland, Oregon, and Albuquerque, New Mexico, apartment managers charge potential renters a non-refundable fee just for "processing" their applications. This is purportedly to cover the cost of a credit check. However, such fees run between $15 and $50 dollars, far more than a credit bureau charges per credit check. Obviously, they're making a profit from processing your paperwork, and sometimes the profit is substantial. In Albuquerque, for example, apartment managers within a mile of each other will charge widely varying fees, from a low of fifteen up to fifty or more dollars, and obviously those charging more are running little businesses on the side, making money from just "processing" applications.

Some aren't satisfied with this, and seek to increase their "business" by accepting applications from inexperienced young couples they know cannot qualify. Some encourage their victims to apply even though they know they have no vacancies at the moment, because they want the processing fee and know the applicants will fail the credit check.

Scholarship Frauds

This is a variation on the fraudulent employment scams. A company advertises that it can find your son or daughter a scholarship, and may even "guarantee" it, provided you pay their fee up front. The advertisement may be in a publication, or it may arrive in the mail. Keep in mind that marketing companies sell lists of teenagers to anyone who pays the fee, and that your child's name and age may be on one or more such lists.

The ad, especially if it's a direct-mail brochure, may promise substantial scholarships in glowing terms, implying that your child's academic standing or your family's income level won't disqualify him or her. This type of claim is so contrary to the usual requirements for scholarship applicants that it should immediately make you suspicious.

What the company delivers is another story, usually a list of scholarship sources to which your son or daughter must apply and with no more chance of obtaining a scholarship than someone who had gone about it the regular way.

Protecting Yourself

Always be suspicious of any advertisement offering scholarships for a fee, especially if it's to be an up-front payment and not a contingency fee. Before answering any such advertisement, check it out both with the local Better Business Bureau, and with the guidance counselor at your son or daughter's high school. Keep in mind that there are legitimate sources of information regarding sources for scholarships, and that this information is available free of charge at your child's school, the local library, and the registrar's office at the college of choice.

Fake Gems

Years ago, people sold fake gold bricks. One modern variation is the fake gemstone, encapsulated in plastic. The usual mode of sale is by telephone, using a "boiler room" operator. If you bite, and send a check or pay with your credit card number, you'll receive gems sealed in plastic, and to deter you from making a close examination, there may be a warning that the gems will somehow lose their value if you break the seal.

Protecting Yourself

Obviously, never buy valuables, real estate, stocks and bonds, and similar commodities sight unseen from someone who telephones you. When buying jewelry, especially, it's smart to deal face-to-face with an established jeweler in your community. He's going to over-charge you anyway, but at least you'll get something valuable for your money, not a chip of glass sealed in acrylic plastic.

Credit Card Woes

Credit card losses in this country have increased from $125 million in 1983 to $720 million in 1992, for the four largest credit card companies. World-wide credit card frauds are even higher. Counting only VISA and MasterCard, 1992 losses came to almost $1.2 billion.[4] It's clear that credit-card fraud has been increasing, but what many people don't realize is that credit card companies have been making it easy for fraud artists.

At first, credit card companies handed out plastic to practically anyone. Unsolicited credit cards arrived in the mail, until companies realized that mailing plastic indiscriminately invited fraud. Federal law prohibited a credit card company from charging more than $50 of a fraudulent loss to the credit card client, so they had to eat the excess.[5] Simultaneously, credit card companies began using magnetic stripes, which are harder to forge, as security measures, constantly improving the information magnetically imprinted on the cards. The latest wrinkle, by Citibank, is including a digital photograph of the owner in the magnetic stripe.

All of this has gone for nothing, because credit card companies have for several years been allowing merchants to submit payment slips based on the customer's credit card number alone. With a legitimate number, a fraud artist can charge goods and services to an unwitting victim. One of the easiest ways to do this is by ordering goods by telephone. This is an important reason why you should guard your credit card number jealously. Con artists use all sorts of tricks to obtain numbers of legitimate, active accounts.

There have been many types of credit card scams, enough to convince most people never to give out their credit card numbers to someone who calls. A new wrinkle is for a caller to ask you for the expiration date. The "hook" is to promise you that you've already won a prize, and that the company needs only your card's expiration date to "validate" it. If this happens, you can be sure that they've already got your number from another source, and just need the expiration date to assure themselves that your card is still good. With both the number and expiration date, they can add unauthorized charges to your bill.

Another trick is ATM card "surfing." A con artist finds a location from which he can see a customer punch in his Personal Identification Number (PIN) when making a withdrawal. Once he has the number, he obtains the customer's card by picking his pocket, or snatching her purse, then is able to withdraw money from the customer's account.

Credit card information can end up in some surprising places. The Federal Department of Housing and Urban Development contracted with a Federal Correctional Institution near Lexington, KY, for inmates to process thousands of FHA insurance applications, entering the data into a computer. Among the data on the forms were information on applicant's incomes, debts, bank accounts, credit card numbers, and checking account numbers. An investigation led the warden to shut down the operation before any prisoners could take advantage of the information laid at their feet.[6]

Protecting Yourself

Avoiding the hazards of credit card fraud is surprisingly easy, although few people are aware of the techniques. There are, actually no "secrets" involved in defense against plastic card fraud.

The first and simplest technique is not to have any plastic cards, and to carry only cash and/or a checkbook. Many people think that they should carry as little cash as possible, and pay for almost everything with plastic, so that they'll lose very little if they lose their wallets or are ever robbed. This is fallacious, as you stand to lose much more if a thief takes your plastic than if he takes the cash you normally carry.

Many people insist on carrying, if not a credit card, an automatic teller machine card so that they can obtain cash quickly, even after normal banking hours. This works, but leaves the customer open to several other rip-offs. "Surfers" are not the only ones to stake out ATMs. Some armed robbers lie in wait for late-night clients, and rob them after they've withdrawn cash. Others don't expose themselves by remaining near an ATM, but ambush people coming out of bars and other late-night establishments, forcing them at gun-point to go to an ATM and withdraw money.

Two obvious counter-measures if you must use an ATM are to withdraw money during normal banking hours, and to go only to those in supermarkets or other crowded places if you must have cash after-hours. Another is to crowd the keypad while punching in your numbers, to frustrate a surfer.

Another protective tactic begins with understanding the difference between a credit card and a "debit" card. A credit card is access to a "line of credit," which in plain terms means that you may borrow up to your credit limit while using your card. Credit limits can be quite high. A fraud artist who uses your card can get away with ten or twenty thousand dollars, although in most cases you'll be responsible for only fifty dollars of this total.

A debit card, on the other hand, doesn't allow you to borrow anything. Instead, when you use the card, you subtract from an account where you already have money on deposit.

If your reason for keeping a plastic card on your person is to pay for emergency purchases, such as a tank-full of gasoline, to avoid being stranded, you can limit any possible loss by keeping only a small amount of money in your debit card account. If your debit card is for emergency use only, and you refrain from using it for convenience, you can keep your balance very small. In such a case, the most you can lose, even if robbed at gun-point, is the cash in your wallet and the balance in your debit account.

Religious Scams

While the notion of whether or not there is a supreme being is open to different opinions and interpretations, one aspect of it is clear as day: It's a big money-maker for anyone who knows how to exploit it. Traditionally, organized religion has furnished a good living to those who knew how to persuade people that they didn't really have to die at the end of their years, if only they had faith and donated money to the religious leader. This is how, for hundreds or thousands of years, communities have supported religious leaders, providing them with superior livelihoods in return for the promise of life after death.

Some religious leaders, however, got very greedy. They tried to extract more money and benefits than normally provided by the system. During the Middle Ages, selling indulgences was a way for Catholic priests to pick up extra loot. These religious scammers have their modern-day counterparts, the notorious "televangelists."

TV preachers harangue audiences with long monologues, during which they urge them to live the Righteous life and heed The Word of the Lord, always ending with the same appeal: "Send money." However, the record of these TV preachers is dismal. Jim Bakker and his wife faced prosecution for fraud and embezzlement. Bakker went to prison.[7]

Jimmy Swaggart, decrying the Bakkers in his TV speeches, himself plunged down the abyss of a sexual scandal when a prostitute got herself air time on TV by stating that Swaggart was one of her clients, and explaining exactly what his sexual tastes were. Oral Roberts gained ever-lasting notoriety when he announced to his credulous fans that the Lord would take him unless he raised $8 million soon.[8]

Short-Changing

Short-changing has been called the "perfect crime" by authorities in the field of fraud.[9] There's good reason for this assessment. The con artist may be a customer or a clerk, cashier, or teller, and he withholds part of the change during a cash transaction, confident that if the victim notices, he can always apologize for the "error."

There are several ways of shorting change. One is simply not handing over the correct amount. The dishonest cashier simply retains part of the change under his forearm as he passes the rest across the counter to the client. If the client counts his change and complains, the rest of it is right there.

Another way is characteristic of ball park and street vendors. The vendor keeps a short stack of dollar bills in his hand, ready to count and to hand over to the customer. The trick is that one of the bills he hands you, after careful counting of their ends, is folded over, so that he counted one half of it first, then counted the folded half. The result? You're short a buck if you just put them in your wallet.

Another short-changing technique, this time with coins, is for the cashier to count each coin as he drops it from one hand into the other. Then he inverts his hand and drops the change into your hand, you think. What he's actually done is to "palm" a coin or two, depending on you to drop your change right into your pocket, without counting it again.

A particularly effective technique is the marked bill, which a dishonest customer uses to con a cashier. The customer in a busy line hands the cashier a ten-dollar bill, and when the cashier makes change for ten dollars, claims he gave the cashier a twenty. When the cashier calls the manager, the customer insists that the bill he handed over was a twenty, and that he can identify it because it had a bank stamp, telephone number, or other unique identifying mark on it. The manager picks up the top twenty-dollar bill in the cash drawer and finds the mark on the back. Faced with this unequivocal evidence, the manager hands over another ten dollars. The trick, of course, is that the trickster's confederate was in the line right ahead of him, and paid for his purchase with the marked twenty.[10]

Protecting Yourself

When paying in cash, always watch the cashier carefully, and count your change every time. Part of the con depends on practical psychology. The cashier depends on customers in a long line trying to avoid holding up the line, and pocketing their change without counting.

Here are some tell-tale signs that alert you to short-changing:

Watch for the vendor who counts your change by merely flipping the ends of the bills, instead of fanning them out or laying each one on the counter. This is the way the folded-bill con works.

Long lines of impatient customers. This is the psychological set-up for short-changing.

A chatty clerk may just be distracting you, hoping to slip you short change while your mind is on the conversation. The innocent question, "How are you today?", sometimes isn't as innocent as it seems.

The bottom line is to count your change, always, always, always, and remain especially alert during the few seconds a cash transaction takes place. If you're the customer, watch for a pattern. One incident can easily be an honest mistake, but several mistakes in favor of the cashier show unequivocally that he's scamming his customers.

Supermarket Scanning Errors

Laser price scanners, now widely used in supermarkets, never make "mistakes." They ring up the price programmed into them by their operators. Of course, some customers notice that from time to time the wrong price appears. The critical question is whether mistakes are in favor of the store, the customer, or a bit of both. Obviously, when they're consistently in favor of the store, watch out!

Protecting Yourself

Remain alert. If you keep an eye on the scanned price, and compare it with the price sticker on the item, you'll spot discrepancies and call them to the cashier's attention. Keep in mind that stores do not usually make "errors" on sale items, but other items not on special, which customers are less likely to notice. Supermarkets featuring "specials" also low-ball customers by raising prices on some items not on sale, thereby making back whatever profit they've sacrificed on their "specials." They're not lowering prices from the goodness of their hearts.

A special tip-off is when supermarkets do not put price stickers on individual items. The price may be on a sign clipped to the shelf, but by the time you reach the check-out counter, you'll probably have forgotten some of the prices. This creates a perfect set-up for scanner scams. Be especially alert when a supermarket doesn't ticket individual items, and mark the posted prices on your shopping list. If you see discrepancies, stop buying at that supermarket, no matter what their advertised specials may be. They're screwing you at the check-out, and overall you'll save money by patronizing an honest store.

Short Cons

One innovative con man who specialized in the short con was Joseph Weil, a legend in his own time who became known as the "Yellow Kid."[11] This extraordinarily innovative con artist usually would think up his own schemes, rather than use the old and shopworn tricks of others.

One such was the eyeglass scheme. Weil bought up cheap eyeglasses with gold-plated frames, and kept a pair in his pocket while pulling his con. He'd travel through rural areas, pretending to sell magazine subscriptions. His magazines would be specially-bound ones, with several pages of large type inserted. Weil would tell his sucker that he'd found a pair of expensive glasses, and would invite the sucker to try them on. At that point, Weil would open the magazine to the pages set in large type, and the sucker would be fooled into thinking he'd just had a miraculous improvement in vision. With that, Weil had no trouble selling the eyeglasses to the sucker.

Another short con attributed to Weil was that of the expensive pooch. Weil would enter a bar with a well-manicured dog on a leash. After taking a drink, he'd tell the bartender that he had an appointment with a banker, and that he would be unable to take the dog with him. He added that the pooch was very valuable, and would give the bartender ten dollars to watch it for him.

After Weil had left, his accomplice would walk in, see the dog, and tell the bartender that he absolutely had to have that dog. The bartender would reply that the dog was not his to sell. The other con man would give the bartender fifty dollars as a "down payment," and tell him that if he could persuade the owner to sell, to contact him at a certain hotel and room number.

Weil would return, stating that his "deal" with the banker had fallen through, and that he was now financially strapped. The bartender would make him an offer for the dog, calculating he'd make a profit re-selling it. They would haggle, but Weil would finally accept the bartender's offer. The accomplice, of course, was not to be found at the hotel.

The dog con is an example of a game that lets the victim set himself up because of his greed. However, con men exploit noble motives as well, as the following example shows:

A short con begging routine was worked by a young Black in Chicago for several years. This boy would work his routine in front of expensive night-clubs, approaching patrons while crying profusely. His pitch was that his mother had given him some money to take himself and several siblings to a movie. His younger brother, carrying the money, had lost it and now they were all stranded without even carfare home. This pitiful story would often persuade the patrons to help by handing over several dollars.[12]

Asking for carfare home is an almost irresistible con when practiced by children. Canny street-smart kids in New York City years ago even bummed carfare from police officers![13]

One aspect of life that lends itself to the short con is death. Con artists, scanning the obituaries, try to collect from grieving relatives for the deceased's "debts," or goods that he'd supposedly "ordered" before his demise. These cons are pretty stale, but con artists still find suckers each year. These con artists victimize people using grief, not greed. Wars are made to order for con artists. During World War II, one fraud operator sent letters to relatives of servicemen killed in action and buried overseas. These letters offered perpetual care for the graves, for a fee.[14] After relatives had sent their money, they never heard from the organization again. The operators had moved on after victimizing many survivors.

A variant is the "International Photo Service," with salesmen soliciting relatives of dead servicemen and offering photos of their graves. The con men did supply photos to those who paid, but they took the photos in an improvised studio where they photographed mounds of dirt. A suitably-marked wooden cross or other appropriate symbol would be inscribed with the name and placed at the head.[15] One extremely profitable aspect of this is that negatives of graves with common names, such as "Smith," would serve for many sales, as it was necessary merely to make additional prints.

Another war swindler solicited money to ship the corpses of servicemen back to their families. Yet another offered to recover dead servicemen's personal possessions for the relatives, for a fee, of course.

Yet another death-related scam is the life-insurance recovery scheme. Following up on obituaries, con artists canvass surviving relatives and disclose that the deceased had a life insurance policy worth a significant amount to the sucker. The con artists solicit small fees to "expedite" payments.[16]

Another way of taking advantage of kind and helpful people is the "lost wallet" routine, in which a well-dressed person claims to have lost his wallet, begs money for transportation, and promises to repay the good Samaritan when he gets home. A variant of this is the check-cashing scheme. This merely involves persuading a stranger to cash a personal check. The scene may be a train, aircraft, or literally anywhere at all. This con depends simply on personal charm, salesmanship, and selecting a credulous sucker.

An oft-repeated cliché is that "you can't cheat an honest man." The basis for this is that some con games pander to the victims' greed. Strangely, even some experts accept this view, making dogmatic statements that victims of con games suffer victimization only because of their moral depravity.[17] The belief that the victim is being victimized because he's somehow at fault has been an intellectual fad during the last couple of decades, and has prompted a "science" of "victimology," which tends to blame the victim at least as much as it blames the perpetrator. This philosophy is attractive to the con man, and serves him well, because it enables him to keep his self-esteem intact by assuming that everyone's as crooked as he, but he's more clever. This is what makes it such a useful lie, and is evidence that con men not only lie to others, but also to themselves.

We've seen several examples of short cons that took advantage of people's kindness and generosity. The short con is particularly valuable for this, because it exploits the noble and impulsive wish to help another human being in distress. Con artists are skilled practical psychologists, and know how to exploit both the worst and the best in human nature.

Protecting Yourself

Short cons, with their appeals to altruism, can provoke a vicious distrust of other human beings. The best defense is knowledge of the common tricks, and applying certain tactical principles that stop con artists while not denying help to honest citizens in distress.

1. Know the common con artist's tricks, and try to keep aware, by reading newspapers and police bulletins, of the ones currently practiced in your area.
2. Learn not to form snap judgments of people by their physical attractiveness, attire, or charm. Con artists are capable of great charm, and can project an appearance of sincerity that is hard to resist.
3. Never give money to a stranger who says he needs help. Never hand over money even if the stranger offers collateral, such as his watch, or writes a check to cover the amount.

4. Don't show the stranger asking for help suspicion, but friendliness. Offer to help the stranded stranger by telephoning his home, or the home of his relative or friend.
5. If the stranger's story doesn't hang together, or if he is unable to come up with the names or phone numbers of friends and relatives to call for help, notify police as soon as he leaves.

High-Tech Frauds

The recent widespread use of cellular phones has led to another type of scam — fraudulent air time for sale. It works like this:

Cellular phones contain a special program and identification chip, called an "E-Prom," which has the customer's name and identification number. High-tech con artists buy cellular phones, a supply of spare E-Proms, and program the chips to mimic the electronic signature of an existing customer. Then they hang around public places, such as subway and bus stations, and "rent" their cellular phones to passers-by. One scheme involved renting air time to South Americans, who used the cell-phones to call their families back home.

Electronic tax return filing can earn big profits for the professional tax preparer who accommodates his clients with "instant loans." However, electronic tax return filing, instituted in 1990, is open to anyone who has the equipment. This includes a computer, modem, and the software for filing the return over the wires.

Just as, years ago, scam artists began mailing in returns for non-existent people made out to require a refund, today they're doing it electronically. One reason for using electronic filing is that the IRS processes these much faster than paper returns, and gets the refund checks out to the taxpayer more quickly, in as little as two weeks. Speed is of the essence in executing a scam, and imaginative con artists are taking advantage of high technology with this scheme.

Convicts testifying before the U.S. House Ways and Means Committee stated that there exist many loopholes in the Internal Revenue Service's security system, making electronic fraud not only possible, but fairly easy. The head of the IRS, Commissioner Margaret Richardson, tried to reassure the congressmen by stating that her agency has new computer "filters" to screen out fraudulent returns, adding that the IRS has already spotted 200 schemes and 3,000 spurious claims in 1994. During 1993, IRS agents uncovered 61,000 fraudulent returns with a total refund value of $110 million. However, an independent consultant estimated that undetected refund frauds could amount to billions of dollars.[18]

The government can protect itself. With thousands of highly-trained investigators, it can track down and punish those who try to cheat it. As an individual, you're far more vulnerable because you depend on the authorities to protect you, but in fact law enforcement officials often cannot. This is why, for you personally, prevention is far more important than coping with fraud after it's been perpetrated on you.

Self-protection against con games is mostly caution and common sense. If you want to become pro-active in the fight against confidence games, see Part IV.

Notes:

1. *Cheating Death*, Edwin Chen, NY, Onyx Books, 1992, pp. 244-246.
2. *Consumer Reports*, February, 1994, p. 74.
3. *Miami Herald*, September 6, 1993.
4. Associated Press, October 17, 1993.
5. It's easy to see why the federal government would pass a law to make things easier for credit card users. One goal of the government is a "cashless society," in which everyone uses plastic cards to pay for everything, thereby leaving an electronic trail that government agents can monitor to learn every detail of your income and expenditures.
6. *Time Magazine Compact Almanac*, p. 29.
7. *Great Hoaxes, Swindles, Scandals, Cons, Stings, and Scams*, Joyce Madison, NY, Penguin Books, 1992, pp. 69-73.
8. *Ibid.*, p. 76.
9. *Sting Shift: The Street-Smart Cop's Handbook of Cons and Swindles*, Lindsay E. Smith & Bruce A. Walstad, Littleton, CO, Street-Smart Communications, 1989, p. 39.
10. *Ibid.*, p. 44.

11. *Hustlers & Con Men,* Jay Robert Nash, NY, M. Evans & Company, 1976, pp. 112-117.
12. *Ibid.,* pp. 122-123.
13. Personal experience of the author.
14. *Hustlers & Con Men,* pp. 128-129.
15. *Ibid.,* p. 129.
16. *Ibid.,* pp. 130.
17. *The American Confidence Man,* David W. Maurer, Springfield, IL, Charles C. Thomas, Publisher, 1974, pp. 3-4.
18. Associated Press, February 11, 1994.

Chapter 5
The Advance Man

An "advance man" is basically a promoter for a traveling road show, such as a circus or rock group. He advertises, rents premises, sells tickets, arranges accommodations, and takes care of the many large and small logistical details for his employer. This system, however, lends itself to wholesale fraud for the bold criminal. One brassy con man cleaned up beautifully at the expense of the residents of a small Oklahoma town.

A certain Mr. Morrison arrived in Wetumka, Oklahoma, one day in 1950. Claiming to be the advance man for a circus, he proceeded to line up the logistics for its arrival. Meeting with the local Chamber of Commerce, he promised Wetumka's business community that the circus would generate a large volume of extra business because people would flock into Wetumka from surrounding areas, and spend money in the town. He mentioned that the circus would buy supplies from local merchants, stipulating that orders would go first to those who bought advertising on the circus grounds. Morrison collected advertising fees, including those for time on the circus sound truck.

Morrison lived high on the hog during his brief stay in town. He ate for free after promising the restaurant owner the contract for feeding circus personnel. He obtained free medical treatment by handing out free tickets to the big top to the local doctor. Meanwhile, local merchants ordered extra supplies to accommodate the big day. Then Morrison left, never to return. He had just "hijacked" the town.

The promised date arrived, but the circus did not. People from surrounding areas crowded the town, but the anticipated circus wasn't there. The head of the farmer's exchange received a package, collect, from the post office. It contained hay and a card from Morrison. He and the others realized that they'd been "had."

They improvised to recover their losses. The mayor proclaimed the day "Sucker Day," and the businessmen gave away their food stockpiles to the crowds. Fortunately, the visitors spent a lot of money anyway, and opening day was a good day for business. Purely by accident, "Sucker Day" became a success. The townspeople forgave Morrison, promising him a place of honor if he returned.[1]

Twenty-four years later, another con man by the name of "Greenberg" used the same scam in a different context to victimize the residents of Lexington, Virginia. Posing as the advance man for Universal Studios, he told the residents that Lexington was to be a location for a Civil War movie starring Burt Lancaster and Audrey Hepburn. He said that he was in town to recruit extras and supporting actors.

Among his tasks was recruiting a starlet who would play a nude scene. He interviewed some of the town's aspirants in his motel room, having them walk in front of him nude. Another female was present at all times, to preclude charges of hanky-panky.

One of the townspeople telephoned Universal Studios and found out that they had no producer named "Greenberg." The local prosecutor rejected this information after interviewing Greenberg. Greenberg, however, had by this time accomplished what he wished, and left town. The checks he'd passed all bounced. He moved on to Hillsboro, Ohio, where residents were more alert, and he was arrested for his scam.[2]

Notes:

1. *Hustlers & Con Men*, Jay Robert Nash, NY, M. Evans & Company, 1976, pp. 270-272.
2. *Ibid.*, pp. 273-274.

Chapter 6
Check Frauds

Check fraud has been with us since the first checks were printed, but various technological innovations have reduced the risk of a check fraud artist defrauding an individual or business with forged checks. Today, many people pass bad checks, but these are often non-criminal in the sense that they do not end up in prosecutions. When an individual merely overdraws his account, then makes restitution, it's not a criminal case. Some people use "check swapping," exchanging large-denomination checks between two accounts, to inflate the apparent value of their assets. As all checks are eventually covered, this is not illegal.

Others, however, cross the line, engaging in schemes that definitely indicate intent to defraud. Check "kiting" is one way.

Check Kiting

There is a system, conceptually similar to the Ponzi Scheme, that a con artist can work to create something out of nothing. Using two checking accounts, he draws upon one, covering it with a check drawn upon the other for a larger amount. Kiting takes advantage of the "float," the time required for debits to pass between banks and be posted. The fraud artist draws other checks on these accounts to cover living expenses and luxury items, which is why the size of the covering checks increases steadily. As long as the scheme lasts, the checks will be good. However, the last check in the series will bounce, big-time.

Protecting Yourself

If you're a banker, there are certain symptoms a check-kiting scheme displays, which serve as tip-offs. Signatures are often the same as the payees, on kited checks. There are likely to be frequent deposits, as the fraud artist races to cover his latest kited check before the float catches up to him. The time any deposit remains in an account is very short, as it quickly goes out to cover a kited check at another bank. Another aspect is an attempt by the fraud artist to break up the visible pattern by making deposits at the ATM, night drop, drive-up, and even using other branches of the bank.[1]

However, there are other tricks, workable with genuine and perfectly legal checks, and these can trap the unwary person who doesn't read the face of a check carefully.

Traveler's Checks

One perfectly legal way to use a scam works with travelers' checks. The Canadian dollar is worth less than the American version, and checks purchased in Canada are in Canadian dollars. Canadian tourists who travel in the United States can often get goods and services for less if a clerk accepts their travelers' checks without looking carefully to see if they're in Canadian or U.S. dollars.

Open Deception

Banks and credit card companies are into a recent trick to trick the unwary customer into taking out high-interest loans. The bank sends the customer a stack of checks he hasn't ordered. If the customer looks carefully, he'll note that the checks are printed with his credit-card number, not his checking account number. Every check he writes on that number will be charged to his credit card account as a loan, and credit card interest rates are in the 20 percent bracket.

Protecting Yourself

One customer got back at the credit card company that tried this trick on him, using their own rules and policies in a way that stung. Upon receiving the checks, he read the fine print, then immediately paid off the entire account. This credit card company awarded its customers one frequent-flier mile for every dollar charged. This customer then made out one of the checks to himself for $10,000, and deposited it in his bank. He then sent the credit card company a check for $10,000, covering the "debt." With the "debt" already covered, the credit card company couldn't charge him interest, but it did award him ten thousand frequent-flier miles.[2]

You may not be able to sting a predatory lender as painfully as in the example cited above, but take note of the first step: read the fine print. That way, you'll avoid getting stung.

Notes:

1. *FBI Bulletin*, November, 1993, pp. 12-15.
2. *Time Compact Almanac*, 1990, Business, p. 46.

Part Two:
Big Cons

Some private enterprises, such as used-car dealers, are so prone to rip-offs and outright racketeering that anyone who is aware of the dangers avoids them if possible. If it becomes absolutely necessary to walk onto a used-car dealer's lot, the client anticipates economic sodomy. Other businesses are not as well-known for their criminal proclivities. Yet others masquerade to avoid the stigma, disguising themselves as legitimate enterprises. We'll scrutinize these types in this section.

Chapter 7
Large-Scale Business Frauds

The reader may be wondering why he and other "little people" are being so severely victimized by the system and other con games, and might even suspect that the "big boys" are immune to this. It's wrong to think that the world's wealthy and powerful people are immune to fraud, especially because some of the brightest minds are working hard to get at their assets. In fact, that's how many of the rich got to be that way.

There appears to be a natural compensating mechanism. Little people don't have many assets, and therefore don't attract the heavy hitters. A con artist would be wasting his time working an elaborate scam on a person of modest means.

Let's get into cases and see what we can learn. We'll find that "organized crime" isn't just a gaggle of swarthy, dark-suited men with foreign accents and surnames. Another fact that quickly emerges is that "white collar crime" overlaps into organized crime, and, indeed, many groups formerly in the more violent forms of organized crime have crossed over into the white collar varieties.

To understand how and what happens, we must first understand why. Let's review a couple of basic facts about crime to lay the groundwork:

1. Criminals aren't necessarily stupid, and only the dumb or unlucky ones get caught.
2. Violent crime doesn't pay well in proportion to the risks. You can steal more with a pen than with a gun, and the consequences are less severe. If you doubt this, remember that Leona Helmsley was released from prison in January, 1994, after an amazingly short sentence. She received a slap on the wrist even after making a statement that only little people pay taxes, revealing an unrepentant attitude.

A man named Phillip Musica had a long and distinguished career at non-violent but very profitable crime. We can only examine what's been documented, but there may be more under the surface.

Musica began in 1909 with a conviction for a customs fraud which involved bribery. The sentence was a $5,000 fine and a year's confinement. A fine and short sentence aren't deterrents against future crimes, but merely among the "costs of doing business."[1]

Musica served his time and started an apprenticeship in what was to become his specialty, "busting out." A "bust-out" is generating income with false inventory and shipping records, to milk an established company dry until it falls into bankruptcy. In 1912, Musica chalked up another conviction, collecting about $500 thousand from various banks using falsified documentation, including spurious shipping and export papers.

During Prohibition, Musica branched out, using a "front" to sell alcohol to bootleggers. Loyalty to his partner wasn't his strong suit, because he ratted on his partner in a deal with the authorities. His partner went behind bars, and Musica walked free.

He walked right into another scheme. In 1923, he assumed a more respectable-sounding Anglo-Saxon name, "F. Donald Coster," and founded a company with an equally respectable name, "Girard and Company." This was another front for diverting ethyl alcohol to bootleggers. His company purchased the alcohol supposedly to make hair tonic, and passed it to the bootleggers. Although this took some juggling of paperwork, the effort was successful. Musica had learned from his previous failure.

He used the profits from this operation to buy into McKesson and Robbins, which was a small "ethical drug" firm with a very respectable history. This began his finest hour, during which he created a classic bust-out using the firm's good name and paperwork. He withdrew money from the firm, issuing checks and credits against phony invoices and inventory slips, using part of the proceeds to speculate on Wall Street.

The bubble burst for him in 1938. Musica shot himself to death after two investigators arrived at his home. His legacy, however, lived long after he died, because he was a truly classic case of fakery from start to finish. Musica became a legend in his own time.

One lesson we can learn from this is that many employers, especially when hiring high-level people, don't check out applicants adequately. The personnel office will conduct a rigorous search to verify that a stock clerk has the high school diploma he claims, but a board of directors will accept an applicant passing under an alias without checking for a criminal record. We'll see more of this as we study other examples.

Another lesson is clear: people often take paperwork at face value. While it's both illegal and technically difficult to forge U.S. currency, other paperwork is even more valuable, and there are no controls over it. An invoice for a hundred thousand dollars or more usually passes without question. Anyone who doubts this need only read the newspaper headlines to see how "defense" contractors steal from the government by over-billing.

Stock fraud has been a long tradition in the United States. Many of this country's biggest fortunes were built on shady tactics. One of the earliest ones to set the pattern was Daniel Drew, who was most active during the middle of the Nineteenth century. Drew was in good company, because other big names were equally criminal. Drew allied himself with Jay Gould and "Big Jim" Fisk in a conspiracy to defraud the railroad magnate Vanderbilt. Drew owned a lot of stock in the Erie Railroad. Vanderbilt wanted to add this railroad to his empire. Drew conned him with a ridiculously simple-minded fraud: watering the stock. Vanderbilt kept buying stock certificates, and as quickly as he bought them up, more appeared. Drew and his co-conspirators simply turned out fresh certificates on a small printing press.[2]

Imposture can be for fun or profit. Sometimes all you need is a title to work the simplest and most outrageous cons. A man using the name of "Lord Glencairn" bought about $100,000 worth of jewelry on credit from a jeweler in Edinburgh, Scotland. He didn't pay his bills and disappeared to America. There, he showed up in Minneapolis in 1871, using another title, "Lord Gordon-Gordon." Living in an expensive hotel, he deposited $40,000 in a bank as cover for his next swindle. He claimed to be seeking land to buy for real-estate developments, which provided him with an "in." Then, as now, a seller will entertain a prospective buyer, and "Gordon-Gordon" collected richly. Landowners ferried him around in luxury while he "inspected" prospective purchases.

He left for New York, supposedly to arrange the money end of the deal, but he preceded his trip with forged letters from prominent (euphemism for "rich") Britishers to various influential (that also means "rich") New Yorkers. This set the stage for his next con. Under the pretext of investing in and "cleaning up" the Erie Railroad, Gordon-Gordon conned the robber baron Jay Gould out of a large stack of stock certificates and $200,000 in cash without even giving him a receipt.[3]

Determined to take a profit as soon as possible, Gordon-Gordon began selling off the securities he'd been given. Gould learned of this, and began doing what he should have done at the outset, checking the "Lord's" references. Gould quickly discovered that Gordon-Gordon was an impostor, and the faker fled to Canada to evade prosecution. However, word of his fakery had spread, and his victims ganged up on him to get him extradited from Canada. There were several false starts and failures, but the impostor knew that the game was up. When his extradition to Scotland, to face the fraud charge, came through, he committed suicide.

A more recent stock fraud had to do with spurious oil fields and oil companies. During the 1920s, oil was the big thing for speculators. The automobile was spreading, and the demand for petroleum products made oil stock the glamour stock, much as electronics is today, and a man named Cox exploited this trend well. He was an experienced con man, having been convicted of forgery, fraud, and mail fraud. Cox's game was phony oil stocks of various sorts. One scheme, known as "stock reloading," was persuading people who had invested in worthless oil stock to trade in their shares, with some cash, for shares in other companies which eventually showed themselves to be equally worthless.[4] Following the pattern, Cox's victims didn't check him out before handing over their money.

The laws governing the stock market are so lax, and they allow for so many manipulations, that it's often hard to find the point where legitimate business ends and fraud begins. The case of Lowell Birrell is instructive.

Birrell, a clergyman's son, was a top-flight law student, graduating from the University of Michigan Law School in the Number One slot in his class. (Remember, criminals aren't necessarily dumb.) He was successful as a corporate lawyer in New York, and as a sideline he operated a conglomerate of breweries.

The crooked part of his life probably began in 1944, when he became friendly with a man dying of cancer. This man, Cecil Stewart, trusted him, and named him executor of his will. Birrell had also become, with Stewart's sponsorship, a director in many firms in which Stewart held stock.[5]

One of Birrell's tactics was to buy up companies with borrowed money, then pay off the loans with money embezzled from his new acquisitions. He used several techniques to boost his companies. One was to prime the pump at the stock market by buying up some shares. Another was planting and passing out lavish "inside information" that persuaded speculators to invest in his promotions. One of his techniques for planting information was to throw opulent parties for gullible media people, who then printed his material as the truth.

Birrell also used other methods. In collaboration with two other swindlers, Virgil Dardi and Alexander Guterma, he sold millions of dollars' worth of stock through "boiler room" operations, in anticipation of today's sleazy "telemarketing" techniques.

Birrell was very clever. As a lawyer, he knew precisely the weak points of the Securities and Exchange Commission's regulations, and he slipped agilely through the loopholes. Because he used multi-layered schemes, almost impossible to understand because of their complexity, the investigation alone took a decade. By 1957, Birrell knew that he was in danger of being arrested. He fled to Brazil, taking at least three million dollars in cash with him. He lived the high life for six years, then inexplicably returned to the United States to face the charges. The case dragged through the courts for several more years, and finally in 1970 Birrell was sentenced to two years in prison. From this, it's clear that crime pays, if you're clever about it.

The United States has no monopoly on con men in general, or business frauds in particular. A quick review of the career of Ivar Krueger, the Swedish "Match King," shows how Europeans were taken in, despite their purported sophistication.

Krueger was actually a mechanical engineer by profession, which shows that he had brains. He worked in the United States, for the Fuller Construction Company, helping to erect the Flatiron Building and Macy's Department Store along the way. In 1907, he went back to Sweden, and founded the construction firm of Krueger & Toll in alliance with a partner of the latter name. Construction was not as absorbing an interest as acquisition, and he bought up all of the match companies in Sweden. By 1917, he had cornered his country's match business.

With this track record, he persuaded two Swedish banks to lend him 60 million kroners for further expansion. He got further capital by what turned out to be a very cheap trick. He forged Italian bonds, and kept the forgeries in a Stockholm vault. Using these as collateral, he raised more money by selling stock in Krueger & Toll, which by this time had become merely a holding company.[6]

Krueger did several things with the funds he raised, such as buying up match companies in various countries, and lending money to debt-ridden governments, such as the French and Greek ones. In return, these countries awarded him match manufacturing monopolies. Through all this, he kept his investors happy by paying large dividends.

Basically, Krueger played a Ponzi scheme and paid out dividends from what he raised in loans and "investments." During the economically wild and inflationary 1920s, he was able to pyramid his earnings without running into any walls. However, time ran out on him with two developments. The loans for which he'd used the bogus Italian bonds as collateral came due. Then, the 1929 stock market crash and ensuing depression destroyed his chances of keeping afloat by more pyramiding, and he began defaulting on his loans.

Some people are reluctant to admit that the emperor wears no clothes, and Krueger's creditors and investors took a long time to realize that their whiz kid was a fraud. Krueger lingered on, still living the high life, until 1933 when he committed suicide.

A more recent example of multi-national crime is the curious incident of the Bank of Sark.[7] Sark, off the coast of France, is one of the Channel Islands. Sark's government is primitive, although under British rule, which made it easy to set up a flim-flam. Strangely, the Bank of Sark was not located on that island. Its assets, such as they were, sat in St. Peter Port, on the nearby island of Guernsey, where it was also chartered. Its facilities included a rented office on the third floor in a small three-story building, a rented telex machine, a rented post-office box, and some furniture. This served as a base for many far-reaching frauds.

A falsified balance sheet showing $72 million in assets for 1969 was the next step. Another was the creation of a fictitious mutual fund, known as the "First Liberty Fund," and headquartered at the same address as the Bank of Sark. It sold its stock mainly to Europeans, because it had not filled out the required paperwork with the U.S. Securities and Exchange Commission. It had, however, some impressive and lavishly printed paperwork.

What had begun merely as a paper bank grew and grew. Operators traded the spurious First Liberty Fund shares for real assets. Other con artists used bank drafts from the Bank of Sark to establish checking accounts and to pay bills. In Colorado, another operator allowed a construction company in financial trouble to use some First Liberty Fund certificates as collateral for a loan to provide "front money." There was, of course, a fee for this service, and it came to $30,000 in real, bona-fide, U.S. currency.

In 1969, a man calling himself Wesley Alexander deposited drafts from the Bank of Sark with a bank in Dallas, Texas. The drafts totaled $320,000, credited to Alexander's account. Alexander then withdrew the entire amount, but the money was not forthcoming from the Bank of Sark. In February, 1970, Alexander dropped off another draft, for

$185,000, made out on the Bank of Sark at Moody & Company in Galveston. Moody took the precaution of sending a Telex to the Bank of Sark to verify the validity of the draft. The reply confirmed that there was enough on deposit to cover the draft. Several other deposits of these worthless drafts took place in Texas and Louisiana that year.

Contrasting with these huge amounts, there were also small-scale efforts to use Bank of Sark drafts as negotiables. A company in Denver paid its phone bill with Bank of Sark drafts, as did a swindler in Kansas City. Another man used the drafts to buy four cars. Braniff Airlines received drafts to pay for flights booked on their credit cards.

This example shows how it's possible to build a house of cards and live in it. Con artists set up a totally phony "bank," in a remote location, and by following the conventions of issuing the right sort of paperwork were able to build up a huge amount of money from a starting point of zero. This proves the point, which we'll recall and emphasize several times, that it's easy to pass counterfeit, as long as it's not the country's currency. A swindler can print stock certificates, certificates of deposit, balance sheets, and financial statements, and parlay them into a small fortune by bilking experienced businessmen who should know better.

Smaller businessmen are also victims of scammers, for several reasons. First, they're more eager for growth financing, which they may not be able to obtain from a financial institution. Secondly, small businessmen lack the time or resources to check out carefully the people with whom they're dealing.

One businessman in Redondo Beach, CA, was seeking investors to finance a hazardous-waste business. A financial consultant offered to help him find investors, and he paid $19,000 in the hope of obtaining $1.2 million financing. This ring, soliciting finder's fees from businessmen, had bilked the Redondo Beach businessman and two dozen others of more than $230,000 with this scheme, according to a January, 1993, federal indictment.[8] A sidelight of this case is that the fraud artist's criminal record dates back to the Bank of Sark scheme.

Another fraud aimed at small businessmen, or aspiring businessmen, is the fake business opportunity scheme. The scammers offer to set up the victim in a new business, such as the portable heart-monitor scheme investigated in Broward County, FL. After collecting the fee, the scammers never deliver.

Not all scammers playing the finder's fee game ask for large sums of money, at least not at the outset. Some ask only for modest expenses, which can be as little as a few hundred dollars. They then play the "salami-slicing" game to induce the victim to keep paying, collecting a few hundred dollars at a time for current "expenses."

Big business fraud hasn't necessarily diminished during the last few years. Two old and previously respected Wall Street firms, Drexel Burnham Lambert and E.F. Hutton, are history after large fines for securities fraud drove them under. Another firm, Salomon Brothers, barely survived after Michael Milken used them as a vehicle for his junk-bond scheme. A medical device supplier, C.R. Bard, paid a $61 million fine for fraud in 1993.[9]

Protecting Yourself

If you're a small businessman, you can, and should, make at least a cursory investigation of any scheme put to you by people you don't know. Be careful even if you do know the people involved.

Always ask for references, and/or a list of satisfied clients. Just as scammers leave unhappy people behind them, upright businessmen leave behind customers who can testify to their satisfaction. Be suspicious if these references are far away or otherwise inaccessible.

Check with the local chamber of commerce, or the Better Business Bureau. State agencies can also help, especially those regulating insurance or securities. There's a central database called the "Central Registration Depository," with over 400,000 listings of individuals involved in securities and other businesses. Included are those with criminal actions against them.[10]

Finally, ask for receipts when an individual asks for reimbursement. Check the dates and places on the receipts for discrepancies. After all, if an investment counselor states that he made a trip to Atlanta on your behalf, he should not be turning in a hotel receipt from Buffalo.

Yes, Virginia, Crime Pays

Does crime pay? You bet it does, especially if it's big enough! Lowell Birrell is a good example of how well it pays. Even if we count only the three million that Birrell took with him to Brazil, ignoring his high income through the several decades preceding his flight, we see that his two-year prison sentence was compensated at the rate of $1.5 million per year!

As we see repeatedly in this book, and by reading current headlines, big-time swindlers tend to receive mild sentences. Michael Milken and Ivan Boesky received slaps on their wrists, a couple of years in country-club prisons known derisively as "Club Fed," not the hard time in maximum security that lesser lawbreakers receive.

Although several of the swindlers cited here took their lives when exposed, this is not the typical end for fraud artists. Those who killed themselves had had many years of very good living before the end. By contrast, the poor but honest person will die with a clear conscience, after a lifetime of hard, demanding work and few rewards.

Notes:

1. *Hustlers & Con Men*, Jay Robert Nash, NY, M. Evans & Company, 1976, pp. 306 and 308.
2. *Ibid.*, pp. 6-7.
3. *Ibid.*, pp. 13-14.
4. *Ibid.*, pp. 205-206.
5. *Ibid.*, pp. 208-212.
6. *Ibid.*, pp. 250-255.
7. *The Fountain Pen Conspiracy*, Jonathan Kwitny, NY, Alfred A. Knopf, 1983, pp. 22-39.
8. *Wall Street Journal*, January 12, 1993.
9. Knight-Ridder Newspapers, February 7, 1994.
10. *Wall Street Journal*, January 12, 1993.

Chapter 8
Insurance Frauds

Insurance frauds operate in both directions — insurance companies rip off their customers, and some customers take advantage of opportunities to rip off insurance companies. The difference is that insurance companies have staffs of investigators to combat the little guy trying to rip them off, while the solitary client is almost defenseless against the predatory insurance company.

Even "legitimate" insurance companies regularly work scams upon their customers. Policies written in fine print, with obscure language making it hard for a customer to understand what is covered and what is "excluded," contribute to the huge amount of money insurance companies take in, and keep. Insurance companies expect their premiums on time, and threaten to cancel anyone who doesn't pay promptly. Claims, on the other hand, take almost forever to collect. However, this is standard practice for insurance companies operating within the law.

Why do insurance companies regularly get away with so much? One important reason is that state regulatory agencies are in bed with the people they regulate. Investigation of customer complaints takes a long, long time. Regulatory agencies are short-staffed, and only the squeakiest wheel gets attention.

Typically, state commissioners of insurance are political appointees, and insurance companies wield tremendous influence with those making the appointments, where it counts. Insurance companies are wealthy enough to make large campaign contributions and buy some legislators.

In some cases, state legislators are insurance agents themselves, such as Arizona legislator Gary Richardson, of District 27. It's legitimate to question the objectivity of a legislator voting on a bill relating to his means of livelihood.

The field is ripe for fly-by-night insurance frauds. One is the fake medical plan, that covers you for a modest premium of 25 cents per day or similar nominal amount, and promises to pay $75 per day for hospitalization. Seventy five dollars per day doesn't cover much at today's astronomical hospital charges, and such plans are truly legalized rip-offs. One "medical coverage plan," was aimed at travelers, purporting to reimburse medical expenses while away from the regular HMO or other health care provider. When one client tried to collect for a $70 medical bill, she found that the fine print precluded her getting a cent.[1]

A major problem is the insurance company which becomes "insolvent," and can no longer pay claims. This doesn't happen by accident, as insurance companies have a record of stability. When a company collapses, there's a 30 to 50 percent chance it's by design, with the operators making off with their policyholders' assets.[2]

The way they do it is by a system of creative bookkeeping known as "premium diversion." This involves generating faked and inflated operating expenses, which then eat up the premiums so that there's very little left when the claims start coming.

Money diverted goes for high living, in the guise of "travel" and "entertainment" expenses. Some of it may be laundered into private accounts in the name of company officials. Lodging surplus funds in off-shore accounts makes them harder to trace when investigators start examining the books, and provides nest-eggs for the insurance scammers evading prosecution by fleeing the country.

Some fraudulent insurance companies are based off-shore, where regulations are more lenient than in the United States. As a simple practicality, collecting from a foreign company is more difficult than collecting from one in the same city or state.

Protecting Yourself

The most obvious step is to make do with as little insurance as you can, because at best, you're not standing on a level playing field. Several ways in which you can avoid the worst rip-offs are:

Don't be impressed by fancy company names and fancy printing on certificates. Check to see if the insurance agent and the company he represents are licensed in your state. This is no guarantee of satisfaction, but it screens out the worst rip-off artists.

Check at your local library to see if the insurance company has a satisfactory credit rating. Best's, Moody's, and Standard & Poor's are nationally recognized reporting companies. However, keep in mind that these reports tell you only if the company is financially stable. They say nothing about how well or how promptly they pay off claims.

Check to see if the insurance company is listed in any issues of *Consumer Reports*, which occasionally rates customer satisfaction with insurance policies.

Notes:

1. Personal account related to the author by the victim.
2. *U.S. News & World Report,* May 24, 1993, p. 48.

Chapter 9
Mail-Order Scams

We've had many mail-order frauds in this country, and unfortunately, various types of mail cons appear to be a growth industry. The reason is that the potential and actual returns from a widespread mail-order scam make it worth risking prosecution for many crooked entrepreneurs. Despite U.S. Postal Inspectors 98 percent success rate in prosecutions, higher than that of any other federal police agency, mail crooks are still thriving. Let's take a look at why, then examine specific types of frauds, and end the chapter with a look at what you can do about it.

Dishonest techniques in mail fraud have diffused into "legitimate" mail-order businesses. The proliferation of junk mail had caused a problem for mail-order sales organizations: how to keep the addressee from pitching the envelope into the round file. A variety of ingenious tricks have surfaced to capture your attention and impel you to open the envelope. Some envelopes are designed to look like official government envelopes, and others have a gaudy promise that you've just become a millionaire printed on the outside. Yet others are much larger than standard size, to catch your attention.

Mail-order is big business, over fifty-four billion dollars a year. *Consumer Reports* states that about one percent of mail-order offers are fraudulent. This, however, is only a subjective estimate, and when we consider offers that are legitimate, but pitched in a dishonest way, that estimate increases.

Misrepresentation

One example of fraudulent merchandise is "solid copper" cookware that isn't. A company selling Philippe-LaFrance cookware advertised a 32-piece set, but those who sent in their $29.95 got four pieces and "discount coupons" for the rest, at a total price of $150. The cookware wasn't even solid copper, but copper-plate. This offer resulted in a prosecution.

Send away $19.95 for growth tablets, and you'll allegedly increase your height by two to four inches in a ten-week period, or sooner. Do you believe this claim? If you do, send all of your money to me, in care of my publisher. If you don't take this ad at face value, you can be sure that enough of your fellow citizens did to make it worthwhile for someone to keep running the ad in a magazine.

The Arizona Institute of Bioelectronics sold a "Solar Powered Necklace" for $19.95 and $1.50 postage and handling. This device, on a metal neck chain, allegedly collects the sun's energy and distributes it through your body to revitalize you. How? I don't know. Do you believe it?

Other types of misrepresentations relate to freebies that aren't free. One ad, for example, promises FREE small vials of famous perfumes. The perfumes are "FREE," but there's a shipping and handling charge of one dollar per vial. Cute.

Contests and Sweepstakes

Magazine publishers and publishing house liquidators use contests to entice people to buy. They use mail solicitations with several come-ons. One type is the window envelope through which you see something that looks like a check. When you open it, you find that it's merely a voucher printed on check paper.

Another is the large-size envelope that gaudily proclaims you to be a "finalist" in a contest you don't remember entering. The papers inside mention an outlandish sum of money[1] if you just sign and return the document RIGHT NOW! By the way, an order form for books and magazines is included, although the ad states that no purchase is necessary to win. However, the return envelope has a space to check if you did include an order, implying that envelopes received go into two different bins.

Another type of come-on is the printed statement:

"JOHN SMITH IS THE GUARANTEED WINNER OF $1,000,000"

Underneath, in small type, is the qualifier:

"If your winning number has been selected."

This is good reason to read the small type, even on the outside of an envelope.

Some scams hook you by phone, if you let them. One goes like this:

A voice tells you that you've "won" a prize. To receive your prize, you must pay for shipping, handling, insurance, etc., and you agree to accept it C.O.D. from the post office. When the postal carrier delivers it, you hand over the money, then open the box. That's the moment of truth, and you discover that its contents are not what you'd been led to believe. The postal carrier, however, has already left with your money, and the telephone scammer has "GOTCHA!"

In part, you owe your fleecing to a person named Anthony Edwards, who started a bold form of this scheme in 1981, at the tender age of 17. His "winners" paid for boxes of sheet rock, which led to the common term, "rock box scam." Edwards received an 18-month sentence in federal prison for his frauds, but he earned two million dollars with them. Other fraud artists, encouraged by this level of return and the slap-on-the-wrist, imitated Edwards.

The 900-number Scams

One of the worst scams, because it's legal and currently impossible to prosecute, is the contest winning notice that entices you to phone a 900-number to find out what you've won. It's legal because there's no deception. The promoters know that some people do not read the fine type, and that some others have such poor judgment that they don't realize that the odds against their winning any significant prize are astronomical.

The 900-number is a telephone company service for the subscriber that charges you, the caller, a fee per minute to call the number. 900-numbers are used by telephone sex fantasy services, and other businesses that provide information by phone. The fine type in the mailing you receive tells you how much it will cost you per minute to call the 900-number listed. Generally, charges are in the three dollars per minute range.

When you telephone the 900-number, you don't get through right away. There's a carefully calculated system of delay, designed to keep you on-line to run the bill up to more than a dollar or two. You'll get put on hold, asked to verify your notification by reading off an identification number, asked your name, address, and telephone number, and other details to prolong the call. In the end, you may win a nominal prize, such as a check for one dollar, but you'll have spent twenty, thirty, or forty dollars for the 900-number call.[2]

Personal Devices

Some personal devices are made for suckers. Obvious evidence of this is that the victims hardly ever complain. Personal devices include baldness cures, penis enlargers, bust developers, and the like.

It's an unfortunate fact that most such devices and "cures" are scams. However, the victim's not likely to report to a postal inspector that he bought a device to enlarge his penis, which he considered inadequate.

Confusing the picture is the obvious fact that a few of them work, although not as well as their users would like them to. There is a prescription baldness "cure," which works in a small proportion of males. Penis enlargers, the well-known vacuum pumps, also work, but not well. The main reason their performance is disappointing to most users is that the instructions with the devices are inadequate, neglecting the most important principle of use: prolonged and regular use produces some results, while intermittent or occasional use does no good.

Hard-core sex magazines, however, carry ads that are more honest, promoting breast and penis enlargers as sex toys, as they do vibrators. "Adult" shops also carry such devices, and some vacuum pumps incorporate vibrators, making them overt sex toys. In that sense, such devices are legitimate, because some people get off with mechanical devices, and in that sense, the devices fulfill the advertisements' promises.

Avant-Garde Media, Inc.

Avant-Garde is a New York-based outfit begun by Ralph Ginzburg, erstwhile publisher of *Fact* Magazine. *Fact* was the publication that purported to tell the truth, implying that the rest of the media were merely telling lies. One of *Fact's* projects during the 1960s was to poll a couple of thousand psychiatrists regarding their opinions of Senator Barry Goldwater's suitability for the Presidency in 1964. *Fact* printed the replies sent by psychiatrists who foolishly thought they could make a diagnosis without examining the "patient." Goldwater instituted a megabuck lawsuit against the magazine, and he won.

After that episode, Avant-Garde branched out to do greater things, resulting in many complaints to the Better Business Bureau, the Postal Inspectors, and various state courts and attorneys-general. The California Supreme Court, for example, enjoined Avant-Garde in 1982 from misrepresenting its merchandise, a pussyfooting way of avoiding a criminal prosecution without actually saying so. The Florida Attorney General issued a complaint of misleading advertising against Avant-Garde in 1983. This had to do with one of the firm's publications, *Better Living*, which despite the name is a sex tabloid. Similar complaints have come from the U.S. Postal Service in

February, 1984, the New York Attorney General in March, 1984, and the U.S. District Court in December, 1985.

Direct Marketing, Inc.

This firm operates under several names, such as Phillipe-LaFrance, a familiar name in relation to the "copperware." This firm sells gadgets by mail-order, usually cheap plastic copies of larger objects whose photographs are used in its ads. Other items sold are "sex pills" which contain only caffeine.

During the 1980s, this company had several encounters with the law. In April, 1982, the United States Postal Service filed several complaints. These resulted in "consent agreements" in July, 1982.

In April, 1983, a subsidiary of Philippe-LaFrance signed a paper for the New York State Attorney General promising not to be bad boys again. The problem this time was that they were taking the money, but not shipping the goods.

In April, 1984, three of this firm's officers pleaded "guilty" to criminal charges involving mail fraud in the guise of a fake charity. In November, 1984, one of the defendants pleaded "guilty" and, in a rare case of a sentence actually being imposed, got a ten thousand dollar fine and four years in prison, but suspended. Another, after a "guilty" plea, received a one-year sentence, again suspended, a two thousand dollar fine, and was sentenced to perform 500 hours of "community work." Heavy sentences, right?

Fake Laundry Bills

Fraud artists show an almost unbelievable amount of ingenuity and creativity. One recent scammer who came to light sent letters to thousands of restaurant owners in at least 21 states, claiming that his clothes had been soiled by a waiter spilling something at the restaurant, and asking reimbursement of a $9.20 cleaning bill. This fraud artist was very smart, asking only for a small sum, and depending on mass mailing and many responses to earn him money. Authorities stated that, by the time of his arrest, this fraud artist had received over

500 responses at his post office box, and they suspected that he had other addresses for this scam.[3]

Merchandise "Notification"

"Merchandise notifications" are still in vogue. One piece of presorted mail, purporting to come from an "appliance warehouse" in Bohemia, New York, but actually postmarked Kansas City, MO, was designed to look like a notification that merchandise was being held in a "secured depot," merely awaiting "shipping authorization." The envelope and notification slip were printed in black and medium blue ink, as if the entries had been hand-written. The entries were intriguing, designed to arouse curiosity. One was for a merchandise number; another for insured value, which was over $100. Fine type stated that "For your protection, insurance is provided at three times replacement value." A panel labeled "Contents" was maddeningly unspecific, with items "Household," "Personal," and "Misc." checked off.

Instructions on the slip made it clear that the recipient had to return the notification within 11 days, with $19.87, "to speed motor delivery to you." A sense of urgency was provided with the statement: "Failure to respond means that the merchandise being held for you will be released to someone else. Return this claim notice within 11 days!"[4]

Law Enforcement

Many frauds are hard to prosecute. Some are hard to explain to a jury, and this is the bottom line for the prosecutor seeking conviction. Others involve too little money to be worth prosecuting.

One option for prosecutors is using a "consent agreement." A consent agreement or "consent decree" is a piece of paper that says, basically, "Without admitting guilt, I promise not to do it again," and is a quick and easy way for a defendant to wriggle out of a criminal prosecution.

A consent decree can result during a prosecution against a large firm or wealthy individual who has enough money to hire a battery of lawyers who can tie up the government's prosecutors indefinitely with a series of delaying tactics. Obtaining a criminal conviction, carrying with it a large fine or prison sentence, becomes almost impossible. The prosecutors, facing exhaustion, are willing to settle for a consent decree, which at least prevents the accused from doing it again under the same name. The fraud artist then moves down the street and opens up at another address under another name.

The Mail Order Consumer Protection Amendments of 1983 empower quick and direct action by postal inspectors, and a counter-measure against scam artists. Previously, fraud operators would close down one operation to re-open under another name a few streets away. Under the new provisions, a court can issue an injunction against an individual, depriving fraud artists of the protection of an "alter ego."

Unfortunately, this involves civil, not criminal, action. An injunction goes only so far, and in any event the court has to become aware of the fraudulent business before it can issue a cease-and-desist order. A "blitz" operation can be packed up and gone before authorities can react, which is why fraudulent boiler rooms today are fast-movers.

Opening under a new name is one of the most effective of bunco artists' tactics. Even brothel operators use it. In Maricopa County, Arizona, when the Sheriff's Office served warrants on whorehouses under a statute permitting their closing, the operators simply moved to another address, forcing lawmen to begin again from scratch. Operators had set up their brothels in house trailers, and needed only to disconnect the utilities, towing the trailer down the street, and setting up at a new address.

The Cost of Doing Business

These new, high-volume mail-order fraud artists take fines in stride. They pay willingly, knowing that the fines are tiny in proportion to the volume of business they do. They consider fines to be "overhead," as simply part of "the cost of doing business," just as bootleggers in the old days used to bribe police as part of the cost of doing business.

Self-Protection

You're just as likely to see these scams, or ones like them, advertised on TV as in newspapers and magazines. It does cost big bucks to pay for a TV ad, but these people deal in millions. You have a number of ways to spot fraudulent offers and protect yourself. Some fraud artists use post office boxes, but a street address is not a sure sign of integrity, as the address may be a mail drop.

There is one sign that's almost a "sure thing" — the price. If you see something advertised by mail-order for twenty dollars or less, it's quite likely a fraud. This is because, right now, twenty dollars seems to be the maximum to charge without running into the psychological barrier of caution.

People spending large sums of money are likely to be more careful than when thinking about a small purchase. Ask yourself if you'd risk sending fifty or a hundred dollars to a company you don't know, for a product or service you've never tried, simply on the strength of a TV or magazine ad. Would you be as careful if the price were five, ten, or twenty dollars?

Twenty dollars seems to be the cut-off line for many people, the threshold of caution. This is why many sleazy offers are priced lower than this. Often, it's just a bit less, say $19.95.

Sweepstakes contests are also suspect, especially if they're operated by an unknown company operating out of a post office box. Ask yourself why a businessman would want to give away millions of dollars in valuable prizes. Businessmen are in business to earn money, not to hand it out with no prospect of return.

Finally, ask yourself about the cost of advertising. If the selling price is five or ten dollars, and you see repeated TV ads for the product, how much is left to put into the product after paying for the ads, shipping costs, and allowing for the profit margin? It doesn't matter if the advertised product is a knife, jewelry, diet pills, or an "air conditioner." It costs something to manufacture. If it looks "too good to be true," it almost surely is!

Notes:

1. Ten million dollars is the sum printed on one Publishers Clearing House document.
2. *Home & Auto Security*, October, 1993, pp. 44-47.
3. Knight-Ridder Newspapers, October 24, 1993.
4. This "notification" arrived at the author's residence just as this book was near completion, showing that mail scams are alive and well in America. A call to the Postal Inspection Service's hot line confirmed that they were aware of it.

Chapter 10
How The Medical Establishment Rips You Off

The central theme of this chapter is that doctors' main purpose is to ensure their affluent livelihoods, at the expense of their patients' pocketbooks, and as we'll document, even their well-being. Through the years, doctors have done this quite well, which is why even today, with doctors crying about lawsuits, government regulation, and the cost of doing business, medical schools are still packed.

A Medical Fraud Glossary

The following terms are not arcane, and some have been part of American English for decades, which shows that medical flummery isn't at all new.

Fee-splitting. Sharing the fee when one doctor calls in another for an extended consultation and collaboration. Akin to "Kick-back." This was one of the topics covered in a report by the American Medical Associations' Special Committee on Medical Practices in 1954.

Ghost Surgery. Surgery performed by someone other than the surgeon of record. The surgeon undertakes to do the surgery, but once the patient is anesthetized, someone else steps in to do the work. This may be a doctor who has lost his license to practice, a medical student, or someone else willing to operate for only a part of the fee the surgeon collects.

Iatrogenic. An illness or condition caused by medical or surgical treatment.

Kick-back. A cash fee paid to a doctor for a patient referral. A specialist pays kick-backs to family doctors who refer patients to him.

Medicalization. Imputing a sinister meaning to a normal physical function or feature, to convince a patient that he needs treatment.

Producer. A doctor who generates a lot of income to his hospital by bringing in a lot of patients for a lot of tests, treatments, and surgery.

Remunerectomy. Unnecessary surgery performed only so the surgeon can collect a fee.

Unbundling. Splitting of medical and hospital charges into the smallest possible components, to avoid easy price comparisons and to maximize profits.

Unnecessary Surgery. Self-explanatory, made easier by the patient's trust in his doctor, and sometimes naive faith that the "doctor knows best."

The Start of Regulation

A century ago, medicine was primitive. Anyone could claim to be a doctor, and many who practiced medicine had insufficient education, and sometimes no education at all. The field was wide open for fraud, and many sharp practitioners took advantage of this anarchy in medical standards.

There was a need for regulation because, just like today, consumers had great difficulty in evaluating medical care. An outside regulatory agency was necessary to squeeze out the overt quacks.

The intention was good; the stated purpose of licensing laws was to ensure that those claiming to be medical doctors actually were, and would be able to provide competent medical care according to the standards of the era.[1] Unfortunately, the medical profession at the time was little better than its rivals, and many doctors simply were not that good. Medical knowledge was still half superstition, and misinformation was widespread. For example, many doctors of that era believed that masturbation caused insanity.

Medical knowledge was primitive, but economic knowledge wasn't. Doctors who joined together in various professional associations found that they could both serve the public and serve themselves. It quickly became obvious that medical care follows the same laws of supply and demand that other goods and services do, with the additional quality of being somewhat "inelastic." Medical care isn't a luxury item, and consumers can't arbitrarily reject it if they need it. This set the stage for jacking up prices, and building a medical care system designed to extract every possible dollar from patients.[2]

The Growth of Protective Regulation

The first step for medical associations was to put in place a system of "population control" of licensed doctors, and to ensure that only *licensed* doctors were permitted to practice. Every candidate was required to attend an "accredited" medical school, to ensure that he received a quality education. The medical establishment limited the number of "accredited" medical schools and the number of graduates, to ensure that doctors did not become too plentiful. Along with this, doctors fostered the myth that they are always "busy, busy, busy." Having patients piled up in their waiting rooms not only built the impression of a "busy" and successful practice, but also gave patients the uneasy feeling that the doctor's time was so much in demand that they were lucky to get in to see him. Today we see doctors, even family practitioners, insisting upon appointments, supposedly to get their patients in and out with minimal delay, but despite this, patients are still being "stacked" in waiting rooms. This is no accident.

The March Toward Monopoly

Part of the effort toward getting a monopoly on health care was squeezing out alternate health care practitioners and facilities. This effort met with varying degrees of success in different states. In some, midwives are forbidden to practice. In others, midwives are allowed, but their powers are severely limited. In some states, chiropractors have a hard time of it. Other states permit naturopaths and other alternate health care practitioners.

This policy of squeezing other health care providers has nothing to do with their competence or the protection of the public. For public consumption, the medical establishment conducts an unrelenting campaign to "educate" the public regarding the "dangers" of bringing their health problems to "unqualified" people. The rationale varies, but the consistent theme is that medical doctors are hostile towards anyone who is competing for patients' dollars.

Part of this campaign involves strong lobbying efforts, not only with legislators, but with writers and editors of popular magazines. We see articles bearing warnings about quackery, and the questionable qualifications of those without orthodox medical training. Even consumer-oriented publications follow the pattern. Some years ago, *Consumer Reports* carried a feature article on chiropractic. The article gave the pros and cons of this system of health care, but two points were obvious:

1. The article was generally unfavorable towards chiropractic.
2. Most of the information in the report came from the publication's "medical consultants." These were conventional medical doctors, who faithfully repeated the orthodox medical view of competitors for patients' dollars.

Finessing Higher Profits

Many people are unaware of how dedicated the medical establishment is to higher profits. Yet, there's documentation that, to doctors out to make big bucks, actual patient needs are almost irrelevant. During the depression of the early 1930s, many economically down-and-out people simply could not afford to go to doctors, and were forced to endure untreated illnesses. The reaction of organized medicine, however, was that the many empty waiting rooms was evidence that there was a surplus of doctors in this country. Their main criterion was the availability of paying patients.[3]

The medical establishment has always followed a long-range program to bring in as much money as possible for its members, with the minimum outlay of effort. Gradually, doctors phased out house calls because with traveling time, these were unprofitable compared to office processing. The excuse for public consumption was that medical facilities and techniques had become so complex that the doctor could not carry all of the equipment with him, and therefore would not be able to provide the best care in home visits.

Because of their prestige, and taking advantage of patients' credulity, doctors were able to persuade patients to accept this, ignoring the obvious fact that most doctors don't keep the specialized equipment in their offices, either. Today, most patients needing X-rays or blood tests are sent to a laboratory, sometimes several miles from the doctor's office. Specialized tests, such as sigmoidoscopy, usually require a specialist, and this means another trip, another appointment, and of course, another fee.

Doctors today take great care to insulate themselves from their patients. Only rarely will the doctor answer his telephone. It's more likely that an answering service will take the call and notify the doctor, who usually has an unlisted number. If he calls the patient back, the doctor's advice usually falls into one of two categories:

1. Give the patient two aspirins, put him to bed, and bring him into the office tomorrow morning.
2. Take him to the nearest emergency room.

The Rise of Specialization

As late as the 1930s, most medical doctors were family practitioners. Today, well over half are specialists, for a very good reason: specialists earn more money for less work. The family doctor takes long medical histories, performs time-consuming physical examinations, and earns less per hour than the specialist. Thus, the rush to specialization.

The character of medical care has changed, as well. Previously, an honest doctor would often admit to his patient that there was little he could do for him. He'd tell the patient with a minor ailment that the best thing for him was rest, because the body would heal itself. This, however, brought in only one fee, and some ambitious doctors realized that they could build up their businesses by pyramiding health care.

The word "pyramiding" has a special meaning in medical care. It means adding layer upon layer of additional tests, consultations, and treatments, by referring the patient to a series of specialists. The growth of medical specializations has had several effects to promote this.

The first is to generate two fees. The family doctor does nothing but refer the patient to a specialist for intensive testing and treatment, but still collects a fee. The specialist, in turn, socks the patient with his own bill. This is one reason why doctors' incomes rose 7.7 percent in 1989, a year when the inflation rate was only 4.6 percent.

The second is to create an opportunity for a "kickback." The specialist charges a higher fee than the family doctor, ostensibly because he's had more training. However, the higher fee provides "padding" so that the specialist can pay a "bird dog" or "finder's" fee to the general practitioner who made the referral. Kick-backs are unethical, and professional associations condemn them, but this is mere lip service because professional associations do practically nothing to wipe out kick-backs.

To be fair, it's important to note that not all doctors collect kick-backs, and that probably only a minority do so. There's no way to be sure, however, because doctors keep this unethical behavior a deep dark secret.

The third opportunity specialization creates is a way to share the risk and blame. The general practitioner can shift the burden of responsibility to the specialist to avoid the danger of a malpractice suit. His defense is simple: he immediately recognized that this was a case for a specialist, and promptly referred his patient to one.

The specialist, in turn, protects himself by a "consultation," calling in another specialist. If the patient seems to be doing badly, getting the services of another specialist shares the blame, if any. The patient's care thereby becomes a decision by committee, because a committee is basically a way of avoiding individual responsibility.

Pyramiding the Profits

With the profit motive an intimate part of American medicine, it's not surprising that doctors go where the money is, and make every effort to pad their bills. For example, doctors with laboratories in their offices tend to prescribe more tests for their patients, according to one government study.[4] Doctor-owned labs performed an average of 6.23 tests per patient, contrasting sharply with the 3.76 tests per patient performed by independent labs. The doctor-owned labs charged an average of $44.82, higher than the independents' $25.48 per test.

All through this the patient pays. The General Practitioner and the specialist do something which would be shady practice and even illegal in other fields: they sub-contract without the client's authorization.

It's easy to imagine the reaction if a contractor built an airplane for the Air Force and included some "extras" not called for in the specification. If the manufacturer installed something not specified in the contract, he'd be unable to collect for it, and probably would be obliged to remove it. This is because the people who administer the contracts for the armed services are professionals themselves, not naive consumers. They often know as much about the product as does the manufacturer, and they can defend themselves in the marketplace. This is true despite the recent incidents of $600 ashtrays and $400 screwdrivers.

The patient, on the other hand, is mystified by much of the goings-on. He doesn't know, and therefore cannot judge, when he's being taken. This didn't happen by accident.

Doctors have an economic interest in keeping patients ignorant. They use exotic language to mystify them, and this process has undergone progressive evolution. Doctors used to prescribe "drugs," "pills," "powders," or "syrups," one- and two-syllable words that everyone understood. Then came the word "medicines," three syllables. This wasn't complicated enough, so today doctors prescribe "medications," with four syllables, but meaning the same thing.

A doctor says "ligate" when he means "cut." He doesn't "sew" up a cut; he "sutures" it. There's no such thing, in medical jargon, as a "cut." It's an "incision" or a "laceration." Everything dealing with medicine or anatomy has a five-dollar word with a Greek or Latin root. The purpose is to keep the patient from knowing what's really going on, and to prevent him from making an informed decision about his care.[5]

One factor that makes this especially sinister is the mutually-protective grouping doctors practice. Traditionally, it's almost impossible to find a doctor who will admit that another doctor made a mistake, was inept, or dishonest. A doctor who testifies in court against another becomes a pariah. When a doctor does speak out against a corrupt practice, others take action against him. Years ago, when Dr. Loyal Davis, a noted Chicago surgeon later to become Ronald Reagan's father-in-law, told a news conference that "fee-splitting is on the increase in Chicago and surrounding areas," the local AMA branch took disciplinary action against him.[6]

Systematic Medical Frauds

If you've seen a hospital bill during the last 20 years you may have wondered how the hospital's staff find the time to list every last pill, box of tissues, and other nickel-and-dime items. This is the key to maximizing profits for both doctors and hospitals. It's called "unbundling," and is the opposite of charging by flat rate. Unbundling means breaking down a bill into its smallest possible parts, and charging for every component and sub-component individually. This is partly to pad the bill, and partly to avoid standardized charges that a patient or his insurance company can compare with others. As we'll see, both doctors and hospitals do this routinely today.

Your daily room rate today merely is for room and board. You'll probably receive a "personal hygiene kit," consisting of a plastic pan, toothbrush, tube of toothpaste, bar of soap, and a few other low-cost items. This will probably appear as a separate item on your bill. If your doctor orders any sort of medicine, pill or injection, you can be certain that each dose will result in a separate listing on your bill, of course at a greatly inflated price. Most of us have already heard of the two-dollar aspirins hospitals provide.

Likewise, your friendly family doctor doesn't just bill you for a office call any longer. He'll bill you for each pill and each shot he provides. A routine physical check-up today no longer consists of listening to your heart and lungs, and asking you if you have any pains. Medicine today is far more comprehensive, and far more expensive. An electro-cardiogram is routine, at an extra charge of course, and the odds are that you'll receive a bill for an array of laboratory tests on your blood and urine.

Stirring up More Business

One obvious fact that spokesmen for organized medicine ignore is that it's much easier and profitable to treat well people than sick people. Recruiting healthy people as patients is called "disease mongering." It's profitable because it leads to more tests and treatments, with little chance of mishap because the "patients" are basically healthy.[7]

One reason we see this is that doctors are "competing for a limited portion of the American population: those who have insurance of some kind."[8] Indigent people don't count. Thus, we see that, in one respect, things haven't changed during the past 60 years.

Calling a normal feature or function a "symptom" of disease is a way of creating a "disease" that generates more profits for doctors. Most people at one time or another feel fatigued, anxious, or feel a pain in a muscle or joint. Convincing them that this is abnormal, and requires at least diagnostic screening and possibly medical or surgical treatment, is an effective way of obtaining business from patients who can afford it.

Another reason is that doctors appear to have a psychological need to make a diagnosis or recommend treatment. One 1930s study by the American Child Health Association surveyed 1,000 children, of whom 61 percent had already had their tonsils excised. The remainder underwent medical examination, and 45 percent were recommended for surgery. Those not needing surgery saw another group of doctors, and 46 percent were deemed to need a tonsillectomy. Forty five percent of the "survivors," examined by another group of doctors, were recommended for this operation.[9]

Let's compare some of the risks: A patient who undergoes colonoscopy to detect colon cancer runs a slight risk of perforation (2 in 10,000), requiring surgery to repair. Surgery has a mortality risk, and for this type of repair it's 5 to 10 percent. Thus, the overall death risk for someone undergoing this diagnostic procedure is one or two in 100,000, which compares very favorably to the death risk for someone who has colon cancer.[10]

Hospitals

Hospitals are the "temples of healing," but the admission charges are very high. They're perfect settings for pyramiding profits and tacking on extra charges.[11] Anyone who's seen a hospital bill recently knows that hospitals charge outrageous prices for everything, and that they relentlessly account for even the most minor items with an inflated entry on the bill. For example, a 16-ounce bottle of hydrogen peroxide, selling for about 85¢ in drugstores, can easily go for $10 on a hospital bill.

If the patient consents to surgery, he leaves himself wide open for sub-contracting. Before the operation, he'll get blood tests, an electro-cardiogram, a chest X-ray, and any other tests the surgeon prescribes. While the surgeon and the hospital must have a signed release for the surgery itself, setting the patient up for these tests requires no permission, except passive acquiescence, and most doctors take advantage of this. The patient gets hit with the bill for the operation, but others get a crack at him as well. The anesthesiologist, chosen by the surgeon, charges for his time. The radiologist, who's done nothing more than to take a quick look at an X-ray, also bills the patient. The cardiologist, whom the patient never sees, but who takes a quick look at the EKG, also bills the hapless patient. A bill for the lab tests, and from the hematologist who looked at the results, also will arrive.

The charges for the tests themselves appear on the hospital bill. Bills from specialists are separate. So are bills from the surgeon and the anesthesiologist. The patient may not even see the anesthesiologist. Before being taken into the operating room, he's been doped up with "pre-medication" and is barely conscious. A nurse inserts a needle into his vein, to drip Ringer's solution into him drop by drop. This isn't necessarily because he's dehydrated and needs fluids, but is simply a convenient vehicle for administering injectable drugs. In the operating room, the anesthesiologist slips up behind him and injects a dose of Fentanyl into the tube, and the patient goes out like a light.

The hospital bill itself is absolutely punitive. One reason why hospital charges are so high is that doctors often own stock in the hospitals where they practice. A doctor may give lip service to his patients' concerns about skyrocketing medical fees, but in reality cares little because he's part of the system, and profits from ripping off his patients.

Doctors, because of their daily contacts with hospitals, are in a good position to know where the best service for the lowest price is available. Despite this, they send their patients to the same hospitals, usually the ones to which they're accredited. "Accredited" means that they have the right to practice there, having supposedly met the hospital's standards, but it often simply means that they own a piece of the action.

The term "producer" is used to describe a doctor who prescribes many tests and treatments. A doctor who is a producer can bring a hospital more revenue per day per patient than one who is slack about scheduling tests and procedures. Of course, hospitals appreciate doctors who are "producers."

Some money-hungry hospitals use a system of rewards for doctors who are hot producers. The Simi Valley Adventist Hospital of Simi Valley, California, gave a $25,000 loan to an obstetrician in return for bringing his patients to it. As an extra reward, he did not have to repay this "loan." Dr. Arnold Relman, editor of the *New England Journal of Medicine*, didn't pull his punches when he stated outright: "The doctor is in bed with the hospital." Additional incentives hospitals provide for "producers include cash bonuses, minimum income guarantees, free office space, and free office and medical equipment. Doctors responding to such financial incentives admit their patients into the hospitals offering them the best deal, not necessarily the best care for the patients."[12]

Another reason why hospital bills are so high is that the patient pays for equipment that is never used on him. Hospitals, and the doctors who control them, are after status and prestige, as are people in other fields. In medicine, part of this striving results in acquiring the latest high-tech equipment, such as a CAT scanner, useful in only a small proportion of cases. The doctor or hospital prefers to use in-house equipment instead of sending a patient to another hospital for a specialized test, but the patient pays dearly. A CAT scanner costs well over a million dollars, and the cost is amortized among the great majority of patients who never see it.

The road to victimization is wide open because the patient, who usually has some sort of health insurance, doesn't look his bill over carefully, and usually doesn't question the charges. Often he gets billed for drugs or treatments he never got, or the quantity is incorrect.[13] Amortization of unneeded equipment factors a hidden cost into his room charge.

Hospitals and doctors foster these abuses by keeping patients ignorant. Usually, they don't allow the patient to see his chart. A patient who asks will likely be told that it's too technical for him to understand. At the same time, the doctor or nurse never offers to go over it with him and explain the technicalities. They're too "busy."

Malpractice

During the last two decades, we've seen a new phrase come into use: "defensive medicine." This refers to unnecessary tests doctors order just to cover themselves in the event of a malpractice suit. Doctors, and their insurance carriers, are concerned over malpractice suits, which have become front-page news during the last couple of decades.

The official line put out by the medical establishment is that such suits come about only because of the raw, naked greed of ambitious and unethical lawyers. They never discuss wrong-doings by doctors that bring about these suits, instead emphasizing the few million-dollar settlements awarded by juries, to justify laws limiting compensation payments.

This tactic works, and it works well. One effect is that many patients do not even know when their doctors are harming them through carelessness or negligence. One study cited by a noted doctor disclosed that, of patients with legitimate claims to malpractice compensation, under 2 percent even filed claims.[14]

The medical establishment's viewpoint is dishonest. Lawyers represent plaintiffs, but the doctors, hospitals, and their insurance companies have their own lawyers to protect their interests in court. The plaintiff's lawyer presents his case, but a jury decides the verdict and a judge oversees the trial. While the judge is typically a lawyer, juries are composed of lay people. While the plaintiff's lawyer gets a percentage of the settlement as his fee, the judge is on salary and the jurors collect only a stipend for their time, whatever the verdict.

The reaction of the medical establishment when doctors are proven negligent in court is strikingly similar to the that of the telephone company when the court-ordered break-up came: "You screwed us good, but now we're going to make you pay!"

Doctors make every patient pay dearly, increasing their fees purportedly to cover the extra costs of malpractice insurance. They prescribe tests, more tests, and consultations to protect themselves. The patient pays for all of this, unable to find out if the tests are really necessary for his benefit, or to cover the doctor's butt.

Unnecessary Treatment

An unnecessary test is usually harmless, unless it's what doctors call an "invasive" test, which means inserting or injecting something into the patient's body. A heart catheter can do damage, but only if the doctor's rough or careless. What does a lot of harm, though, is unnecessary treatment.

Let's take the patient with a cold as an example. Medical doctors have never been able to cure the common cold. Some of them have a cynical saying to describe this situation: "With intensive therapy, a cold can be beaten down in seven days; if you neglect it, it'll go away in about a week."

When the first antibiotic, penicillin, came out during the early 1940s, doctors gave their cold sufferers shots. These didn't cure the colds, as doctors soon found out, but widespread use of penicillin helped breed new penicillin-resistant strains of microbes. Some of these were more harmful, causing more severe symptoms. This is why there's been a constant search for new antibiotics. Abuse and over-use of antibiotics usually does no immediate harm to the patient, but down the road they create more problems.

The program when giving a useless injection works like this: The doctor gives the patient a shot, and tells him to come back in a week for another check-up. This creates three billable items — two office visits and one injection fee. This program is far more profitable than simply telling the patient to go home, drink some hot tea or whiskey, and go to bed. The patient then might go away wondering, "Why did I need to pay the doctor just to tell me that?"

Unnecessary work on your car costs you money. Unnecessary treatment can cause more serious problems. Harried and overworked nurses make mistakes when administering drugs in hospitals. Some overworked and exhausted nurses take stimulants to keep themselves awake, and excessive use can impair their judgment. Transmission of disease is an unpublicized hazard. Your doctor or dentist may have caught AIDS, or more likely the flu or hepatitis, from another patient. Staph infection sometimes runs through hospital wards, spreading quickly because there are so many sick people so close together.

Unnecessary treatment becomes very dangerous when it involves surgery. Any surgery brings with it risks of complications. Over 13,000 patients die from anesthesia-related causes each year in this country.

Other medical deaths are even greater. About 150,000 Americans are killed by medical treatment each year, and over half of these die as a result of doctors' negligence.[15]

The abuse of Americans by their doctors is striking when we compare medical treatment given in other countries. We can't compare American medicine with that available in Afghanistan or Kuwait. Let's look at European countries, where there's every reason to believe that doctors are just as competent as American ones.

It's been known for years that Americans, compared to Europeans, are over-medicated and over-operated.[16] Europeans undergo far less surgery than do Americans. Most Europeans grow up retaining their tonsils, and European women rarely have hysterectomies. Hysterectomies in America have become fashionable surgery, like status symbols. Hysterectomies are also very profitable.

One doctor, asked if he'd continue to practice if he won the Florida Lottery, at that time with a $40 million pot, replied that he would continue to operate, but would perform only medically justified operations.[17]

The problem of unnecessary surgery has existed for decades, or longer. Years ago, one study disclosed that people covered by medical insurance underwent surgery about twice as much as uninsured persons.[18] A study published in the *Journal of the American Medical Association* in 1953 showed that about one-third of hysterectomies were unnecessary.[19]

Another aspect of unnecessary surgery is childbirth by Cesarean, instead of normal vaginal delivery. For some unexplained reason, American women have developed an acute health problem over the last couple of decades, so that now about 25 percent of deliveries are by Cesarean. Cesareans are uncommon in Europe, but they're profitable in America.

An obstetrician earns three to four times as much for a Cesarean as he does for a normal delivery. It also carries with it an operating room fee, an anesthesiologist's fee, and fees for various tests normally done before surgery.

Another reason for the increase in Cesareans is related to defensive medicine. Some women, because of a narrow pelvis or other reason, have a harder time than others during childbirth. The obstetrician has to work harder, too, and if anything goes wrong he fears being liable for not having chosen Cesarean delivery. Some obstetricians routinely advise Cesareans to pregnant patients with the slightest signs of complications. This way, they cover themselves, and the patient pays.

Yet another reason is convenience for the doctor. Labor can begin at any hour, and continue for many hours, regardless of whether the doctor's got a golf date or not. Surgery, by contrast, is easy to work into the doctor's schedule. It's also profitable for the time spent.

Amputating Healthy Tissue

Whether born naturally or Cesarean, if the baby is male, he's likely to feel the knife himself a few days after birth when the doctor (or nurse, in some instances) amputates the foreskin from his penis. Circumcision is a conspicuous example of widespread medical greed, and it's worth examining in detail how American doctors persuade parents to have normal, healthy tissue removed from a baby's penis without anesthesia.

The majority of American males are circumcised a few days after birth, without medical reason, and without anesthesia.[20] Doctors easily obtain parents' consent, because parents don't usually watch it done, and remain unaware of the pain this unanesthetized surgery produces. Doctors and nurses tell parents a little white lie, that the baby's nervous system is too undeveloped to register pain.

Profit is definitely the main motive. A statistical study of circumcision and economic status showed conclusively that boys were circumcised in direct relation to family income.[21]

Infant circumcision is profitable. Today, the typical fee is $300, and the surgical tray set-up is another $100 or so. Doctors keep parents unaware of the risks of serious complications, which outweigh any possible benefits.

The Politics of Circumcision

The politics of circumcision has changed over the years, reflecting changing medical practice. Traditionally, the obstetrician would deliver the baby and perform circumcision if it was a boy. In 1971, and again in 1975, the Ad Hoc Task Force on Circumcision of the American Academy of Pediatrics concluded that there are no benefits to routine circumcision.[22]

Infant circumcision began declining, but the most significant change was that obstetricians largely stopped doing them, partly because the tide of opinion had begun swinging against newborn circumcision. Some medical insurance carriers, such as Pennsylvania Blue Cross, stopped paying for it. Another reason was that obstetricians' malpractice insurance didn't cover surgery on the infant. The importance of this was underlined when, in August 1985, two baby boys being circumcised by two different doctors in Northside Hospital in Atlanta, Georgia, had their penises badly burned by the electro-cautery. One boy had to have extensive plastic surgery, but the other was so badly burned that the only choice was a sex change operation, hormone therapy, and raising him as a girl.[23]

Europeans, with socialized medicine instead of medicine for profit, simply don't practice circumcision, except for small religious minorities.[24] By contrast, American doctors continue to sell circumcision to parents, although the newborn circumcision rate has dropped from about 95 percent to about 60 percent during the last couple of decades.

At this point, it's important to consider the "turf wars" among doctors over who performs which procedures.[25] Doctors scramble to get what they consider their share of the business, which in the context of medical care, can only mean taking it away from another doctor.

With obstetricians dropping out of the circumcision picture, pediatricians were now ready to pick up the business, and in 1989, the American Academy of Pediatrics reversed its view, concluding in a report that "...the procedure has potential medical benefits and advantages..." This report, relying mainly on a statistically flawed study of urinary tract infections in boys to justify amputation of healthy tissue, paved the way for the resumption of infant circumcision by many doctors.

With no solid medical reason for removing healthy tissue, how do doctors continue to justify circumcision? Some claim cleanliness as a benefit, although none suggest mutilating the genitals of baby girls to make cleaning easier. Washing under the foreskin seems to have a high priority, although for some unexplained reason no doctor advocates douching little girls. Brushing and flossing the teeth takes much longer than washing the penis, yet no dentist advises having healthy teeth extracted to simplify oral hygiene.

A strange reason given is to make the boy "match" his father or playmates. This is locker-room conformism, and there's no evidence that leaving the boy natural will cause psychological trauma. Boys also differ from fathers in height, weight, hair and skin coloring, facial features, body build, and other physical features such as eyeglasses and surgical scars. However, no doctor would advise, and no parent would accept, removing a boy's appendix to match his father's appendectomy scar.

Why, then, does circumcision continue as the most common surgery in this country? It's profitable, that's why. As with other surgery, both doctor and hospital get their "cut." A surgeon earns more money than most other doctors, and other doctors such as obstetricians and pediatricians charge more per hour for a surgical procedure than for less radical treatment.[26] Doctors typically circumcise several baby boys in one session, lining them up for this mass-production surgery, and earning a higher per-hour rate than for delivery.

This is why some doctors use the "hard sell" in persuading parents to have their boys circumcised. Ann Conceicao, of St. Petersburg, Florida, refused to sign a consent form for her son's circumcision. Next day, the doctor told her the boy had not been able to urinate because of his long foreskin, and urgently needed to be circumcised. The mother signed the consent form, and the boy was immediately circumcised. Later, the nurse who had been there when he was born came on duty and told the mother she'd seen the boy urinate as he was being born.[27]

Selling Fashionable Surgery

Plastic, or cosmetic, surgery is a perfect example of how surgeons take advantage of patients' anxieties to sell them expensive and totally unnecessary surgery. A quick look in the yellow pages shows clearly how plastic surgeons use the hard sell to recruit patients. We can easily see why plastic surgery is a growth industry in the United States. Today, over one million Americans have cosmetic surgery each year.[28]

It's important to distinguish between cosmetic and reconstructive surgery. One is necessary to repair damage from an accident or injury. The other is merely vanity surgery, strictly fluff and frills. This is why, among medical doctors, cosmetic surgeons are known derisively as "tits and butts men." In 1992, there were about 4,000 members of the American Society of Plastic and Reconstructive Surgeons.

Repairing a broken nose is definitely not the same as cutting away wrinkles. Plastic surgeons seeking extra income strive to make people dissatisfied with the way nature made them. The simple fact is that most of us aren't as good-looking as highly-paid professional models or entertainers, and if we aspire to make ourselves over to be as physically perfect as they are, we're lucrative targets for medical manipulators. They present ideal human faces as examples to imitate, and encourage a person with a blemish to have it removed, or a bump or curve in his nose to have it straightened. A slightly weak chin is a target for a plastic or bone implant. Small breasts are candidates for silicon implants, and silicon implants have caused serious problems years after implantation. The problem has become so severe that the U.S. Food & Drug Administration has challenged the safety of such implants.[29]

Organized medicine, however, fights tooth and nail to preserve its members' incomes. The American Medical Association stated that, despite the risks, women ought to be able to have breast implants, provided that they are informed of the risks. David Kessler, FDA Commissioner, pointed out that the AMA had been overlooking "the serious failings of physicians" using the implants in women without proper informed consent.[30]

Plastic surgeons, like psychiatrists, follow the money. People having cosmetic surgery are more likely to come from higher-income families. The money allure is so great that some doctors cut corners. One doctor in Scottsdale, Arizona, was not formally trained to practice plastic surgery, but had opened a practice in partnership with a board-qualified and experienced plastic surgeon. After his partner's death, he continued to practice, but after several patient complaints, the Arizona Board of Medical Examiners took action.[31]

Criminal Greed

It may appear incredible, but many doctors are motivated by greed, not altruism. Medical men will, of course, deny this completely, and say that lay people, lacking their specialized training, can't understand or judge the need for various treatments and surgery. This may be so. Perhaps medicine is such an arcane subject that the rest of us can't understand it, and unfairly accuse high-minded doctors of merely chasing the buck.

However, even the least-educated and insightful person can understand that, once the patient dies, there's nothing more a doctor can do for him except to continue to send bills. That's what some doctors did, in an effort to milk the system. The Inspector General's Office of the U.S. Public Health Service reported that some Arizona physicians collected fees for treating 1,345 dead people during one year (October 1, 1982 to September 30, 1983) from the Arizona Health Care Cost Containment System.[32] Some of these doctors kept collecting fees for as long as 19 months after the patient's death. Other Arizona doctors collected $1.1 million to treat Indians whose health care was provided by the Indian Health Care Service.

This provides a better perspective on medical greed and how it affects medical practitioners. Keeping the profit motive in mind, we can understand the "knife-happy" surgeon who prefers a radical solution on the operating table to a milder, but less profitable course of treatment.

Publish or Perish

Up to now, we've been looking at how doctors chase the buck. Actually, there's another motivation besides fortune — fame. The medico who devises a new treatment or discovers a new disease will have his name immortalized in print. A quick flip of the pages of any medical dictionary will reveal an array of personalized diseases, syndromes, anatomical features, reflexes, instruments, and treatments. Some examples are:

Alzheimer's Disease, Babinski Reflex, Bartholin's Glands, Bright's Disease, Cheyne-Stokes Breathing, Cowper's Glands, Foley Catheter, Freulich Syndrome, Hansen's Disease, Hare Traction Splint, Huntington's Chorea, Jarisch-Herxheimer Reaction, Kaposi's Sarcoma, Kelly Forceps, Korsakoff's Psychosis, Lugol's Solution, McBurney's Incision, Meniere's Syndrome, Moro Reflex, Parkinson's Disease, Reyes Syndrome, Ringer's Solution, Tay-Sachs Syndrome, Thomas Splint, Tourette's Syndrome, Tyson's Glands, and Vincent's Infection.

Many doctors are eager for fame, but there are only so many diseases to go around. The popular ones are already taken, and it's no fun giving your name to an obscure tropical disease with only 21 cases discovered in all history. The field for new treatments, however, is wide open, offering the best opportunity.

Some crave recognition so much that they'll take certain short-cuts to attain fame. We've already seen the problems with honest medical research, and how some cures which appear useful at first turn out to be over-rated or worthless upon more careful examination. One recent and much-noted scandal concerned a Dr. John C. Long, who had reported startling results in his cancer research. He'd faked it, to the embarrassment of Massachusetts General Hospital, with which he'd been associated.[33]

Long was not unique. Other medical researchers have been caught fudging their research, a phenomenon described as a "crime wave."[34] It's certain that those caught comprise only the tip of the iceberg, because of the closed, self-protective society of doctors. Falsified research has dealt with topics such as psychotropic drugs, cancer, and skin-grafting, among others.

Even AIDS has had its suspicious characters. Dr. Robert Gallo, of the National Institute of Health, claimed "discovery" of the HIV virus in 1985, but it turned out that the sample Gallo had presented was "virtually the genetic twin" of a virus sent him two years earlier by Dr. Luc Montagnier, of the Pasteur Institute in Paris.[35]

John Darsee, a medical researcher specializing in heart disease, falsified his data and published it in about 100 medical articles.[36]

Medical schools, contrary to popular opinion, do not exist to educate new doctors, but are merely vehicles for professors to gain fame and fortune by publishing the results of research. Sometimes, this research is stolen from others. One professor was invited to speak at an international conference. He told his subordinate this, and when the subordinate asked him what his presentation would be, the answer surprised him. The department head told him that he would present the subordinate's research, as the professor had been too busy taking care of administrative details to do any research of his own.[37]

Doctors who falsify their results for the acclaim of their peers are playing games with their patients' well-being and their lives. Falsified information can also have serious consequences for people who are not their patients, but who are treated by other doctors misled by the chicanery.

Another aspect of this chicanery is the doctor for hire, the medical researcher employed by an "ethical" drug company. This sort of employee is paid to get results, because results affect the company's bottom line.

Therefore, the temptation to present favorable results of drug tests, even if they're falsified, is strong for a medical doctor drawing a healthy salary and eyeing an incentive bonus. This is why the U.S. Food and Drug Administration has been progressively tightening its rules in recent years. Today, a new drug must not only be safe, but proven to be effective, before the FDA will allow it on the market. The FDA's rules are so strict because of the pharmaceutical industry's history of peddling worthless drugs.

"Ethical" Drug Companies

About 35 years ago, the Kefauver Committee of the U.S. Senate inquired into why American drug companies charged so much more than foreign producers. Despite rationalizations by representatives of the U.S. "ethical" drug industry, the conclusion was clear: greed.

There hasn't been much progress since then. In some ways, the picture has gotten worse. "Generic" drugs were supposed to relieve the economic pressure on patients hammered by "sticker shock." In fact, the generic label has also served as an outlet for substandard products passed by the U.S. Food and Drug Administration after falsified laboratory tests. Three employees of the FDA's generic-drug division pleaded guilty to accepting $24,300 in bribes from "ethical" drug companies.[38]

Drug companies are required by law to test all new drugs in controlled experiments before the United States Food and Drug Administration allows their release. One medical school professor stated that research projects funded by a drug company were very likely to conclude that the new drug was superior to an older, alternate form of therapy. In other words, drug companies got the positive results for which they paid. There was, also, not a single instance of a drug company funded study concluding that the new drug was inferior to a competitor's product.[39]

Another questionable practice is the intense promotion of prescription drugs. U.S. pharmaceutical companies spend an average of $8,000 per physician in marketing. Some of this marketing includes "lavish parties and frequent-flier points to physicians" for prescribing their drugs.[40]

Abuses by drug companies may bring government controls in the wake of the surge towards government regulation of medicine. Arkansas Senator David Pryor, who stated that "The drug industry doesn't like any plan that infringes on their right to charge exorbitant prices for drugs," released his committee's report, which showed that brand-name drug prices increased over three times faster than generic prices during 1993.[41] Pharmaceutical companies have traditionally justified their high prices by citing the cost of research that they must absorb.

At the same time, a U.S. General Accounting Office study found that Americans are charged 60 percent more, on the average, for prescription drugs than Britons.[42] Interestingly, the GAO report brought out that the older drugs, supposedly with research and development costs already amortized, have the widest price gaps.

A recent development has been drug companies' advertising their prescription drugs directly to patients, as well as the doctors authorized to write prescriptions. One company distributed free copies of a videotape promoting its hair restorer.

Drug companies also enhance their advertising by paying writers to do pieces on their drugs. The writer knocks out an article approved by the drug company, collecting a fee for this, then peddles it to a magazine, collecting a second fee. This practice has spread to the electronic media. Many TV medical reporters are "merely shills for medical advertisers."[43]

Protecting Yourself

How can you keep yourself from being victimized? It's not easy. If you need emergency care, you're at the mercy of the hospital and doctor. The good part is that emergency care is where American medicine performs best. You're not likely to get screwed.

Routine care is the problem, and that's where you can help yourself the most, using several methods.

1. Attitude is your most important defense. Adopt a courteous, but reserved and skeptical attitude toward your doctor. Don't assume

that what he tells you is correct, especially if it involves more tests, treatments, and expenses. Remember that he's the expert, but it's *your* body. He has many patients, but yours is the only body you have.

2. Knowledge is power. This cliché is especially true when dealing with a doctor. If you have some medical knowledge, you're already able to defend yourself against some of the abuses. If you don't have it, get it. There are several ways to do this. Self-study is one. Another is to enroll in a paramedic course at a local college. You can't hope to equal a doctor's knowledge, but at least you'll be able to spot the more flagrant abuses.

3. After your doctor arrives at a diagnosis, and prescribes a drug or other treatment, don't simply take his word for it. Consult a reference book on drugs, pills, and treatments. Go to the local library and start digging. If he prescribes a generic drug, ask him if he's prescribed that particular generic for other patients, and if he's found it to be effective.

4. Always get a second opinion if your doctor advises surgery. Be especially wary if your doctor is the one who will be doing the surgery, because he has a direct financial incentive, or if he refers you to a surgeon. Obtaining a second opinion is more costly in the short run, but an office consultation costs far less than the pile of bills you'll incur if you climb up onto the operating table. Also, remember that with surgery you don't get a second chance. Once you go for it, that's the ball game.

5. Be especially wary of trendy or fashionable treatments or surgery. The latest drug or operation isn't necessarily the best. Also, avoid elective or unnecessary surgery of any type. Cosmetic surgery has risks, and isn't necessary to correct a health-threatening problem.

6. Remain healthy. Good genes have a lot to do with your state of health, but behavior can cause serious health problems, even for those with good heredity and strong constitutions. Try to avoid obvious health hazards. Three significant ones are tobacco, lack of exercise, and excessive drinking, as people prone to these hazards tend not to live as long as others.

7. Get to know the hospitals in your area before you have to stay in one. Keep your eyes and ears open when visiting sick friends, and

ask them how they're being treated. Look over the ward for general cleanliness and order, and pay special attention to the nurses. They, unlike doctors, care for the patients around the clock.

Do they appear bright and alert, going about their duties conscientiously? Danger signs are apathy, poor attitude, and especially physical appearance. Today, when it's common knowledge that excess weight is unhealthy, there are still some nurses with battleship-like silhouettes, who would have trouble passing through the Panama Canal. Excess weight in any sort of medical personnel is not a confidence-builder.

8. Residents of border states have an attractive option in obtaining prescription drugs. They can drive down and buy them in Mexico for much less than their cost in the U.S. Premarin and many other older drugs, for example, are about one-tenth their American retail cost. This makes it worthwhile for residents of metropolitan areas a couple of hundred miles from the Mexican Border, such as Phoenix and Albuquerque, to drive down, because the price savings outweigh the cost of driving.

Another attractive point is that Mexican laws are more liberal than American drug regulations. The person deciding to treat himself can obtain many drugs without a prescription in Mexico. U.S. Customs guards are in practice very permissive, allowing seniors to re-enter the U.S. without even examining their packages in many cases.[44] This makes Mexican pharmaceuticals very attractive to those on fixed incomes.

All in all, you're swimming in shark-infested waters when you go for medical treatment. Be careful out there, and be prepared to protect yourself. Be especially careful of medical quacks, because they do exist. We'll scrutinize these next.

Notes:

1. *The Screwing of the Average Man*, David Hapgood, NY, Bantam Books, 1975, p. 107.
2. *Ibid.*, pp. 108-109.

3. *The Doctor Business*, Richard Carter, NY, Pocket Books, 1967, pp. 58-59.
4. *Wall Street Journal*, March 1, 1989, article by Michael Waldholz and Walt Bogdanovich, "Doctor-owned Labs Earn Lavish Profits in A Captive Market."
5. *The Screwing of the Average Man*, pp. 111-112.
6. *The Doctor Business*, pp. 87-88.
7. *Disease-Mongers*, Lynn Payer, New York, 1992, John Wiley & Sons, pp. 4-7.
8. *Ibid.*, p. 9.
9. *Ibid.*, pp. 30-31.
10. *Ibid.*, p. 12.
11. *The Screwing of the Average Man*, pp. 105, and 114-117.
12. Associated Press, December 2, 1990, article by Fred Bayles and Daniel Q. Haney, "Money, Gifts, Used to Retain Doctors' Loyalty."
13. *The Screwing of the Average Man*, pp. 119-120.
14. *Dear America*, Melvin Konner, M.D., NY, Addison-Wesley Publishers, 1993, p. 15.
15. *San Francisco Examiner*, May 11, 1993, p. A-12.
16. *The Screwing of the Average Man*, p. 110.
17. *Dear America*, p. 30.
18. *The Doctor Business*, p. 88.
19. *Ibid.*, P. 89.
20. *Consultant*, February, 1984, pp. 67-71.
21. *American Journal of Public Health*, August, 1986, Vol. 75, No. 8, article, "Circumcision in the United States," Ann Reid Slaby, MS, MSc, and Terrence Drizd, MSPH.
22. *Pediatrics*, October, 1975, pp. 610-611.
23. *Sexuality Today*, Volume 9, Number 3, November 4, 1985, and Newark *Sunday Star-Ledger*, November 17, 1985, article by Joan Whitlow.
24. *Circumcision, An American Health Fallacy*, Edward Wallerstein, NY, Springer Publishing, 1980, pp. 31-32.
25. *Disease-Mongers*, p. 75.
26. *The Screwing of the Average Man*, p. 109.

27. *Circumcision: The Painful Dilemma*, Rosemary Romberg, South Hadley, MA, Bergin & Garvey, Publishers, p. 157.
28. *The American Society of Plastic and Reconstructive Surgeons' Guide to Cosmetic Surgery*, Josleen Wilson, New York, Simon & Schuster, 1992, p. 13.
29. *New York Times*, April 19, 1991, "Cosmetic Breast Implants Again Cited As Health Risk."
30. Associated Press, December 1, 1993.
31. *Arizona Republic*, January 27, 1991, article by David Cannella, "Scottsdale Physician Faces New Complaints."
32. *The Arizona Republic*, October 23, 1985, p. 1.
33. *Cheating*, J. Barton Bowyer, NY, St. Martin's Press, 1982, p. 423.
34. *Ibid.*, p. 423.
35. *Information Please Almanac*, Boston, Houghton Miflin Company, 1993, p. 545.
36. *Ibid.*, p. 545.
37. Personal communication from a retired doctor who knew the party involved.
38. *Time Compact Almanac*, 1990, Business, p. 56.
39. *Disease-Mongers*, p. 55.
40. *Ibid.*, p. 66.
41. Associated Press, February 1, 1994.
42. Associated Press, February 3, 1994.
43. *Disease-Mongers*, pp. 62-63.
44. Personal experience of the author.

Chapter 11
Medical Quackery

An Associated Press report stated that about 50% of Americans approve of and would seek unorthodox cancer treatments, even though they're not sanctioned by the medical establishment.[1] The article quoted one doctor, a member of the American Cancer Society, as saying that this poll showed Americans' fear of cancer. Being a medical doctor, he did not admit another, equally obvious, fact. Americans distrust their doctors so much that they're willing to place their lives in the hands of others.

With the medical establishment in disrepute, the door's wide open for medical quackery. We've always had quacks with us,[2] but distinguishing them from reputable medical practitioners today is somewhat easier, because we've learned what makes a quack, just as we know more about the medical profession's shortcomings. Comparing the two allows us to make better-informed judgments about their abilities, and to determine whether or not we're being ripped off. We're more knowledgeable, and understand that we can be ripped off by both "legitimate" and unorthodox medical practitioners.

As we've seen in the previous chapter, there are many problems with orthodox licensed physicians. Keep in mind that, whatever their many failings, doctors still have to pass a standard course of instruction, and use drugs licensed by the U.S. Food and Drug Administration. These rules have gotten tighter during the last few years.

As we've seen, today it's not enough to prove that a drug or treatment is safe. It's also necessary to prove that it works the way it's supposed to work before putting it on the market. Many of the quack drugs and treatments have no such proof.

This is still true despite some of the exotic legends we hear about some of these drugs and treatments. One of the most interesting, because of its gut-level appeal, is the one about cancer "cures:"

"The medical profession is holding back on finding a cure for cancer because it's making so much money treating patients with the existing, relatively ineffective treatments. There's a drug available, but the doctors' lobby is preventing its being licensed in this country because they feel it will hurt their business."

Let's look at this line of reasoning closely, because it shows the essence of quackery, the warning signs that can alert you to someone who's trying to rip you off with a fake cure.

The first point is that this train of thought appeals to many people because it has a kernel of truth. Many doctors *are* greedy, and often their main motive is money, not the patient's welfare. As we've seen in the medical rip-offs chapter, doctors earn a lot of money prescribing unnecessary drugs and operations for minor or non-existent problems. They don't need to "lobby" against any effective cancer drug, merely make sure that its use remains in their hands. If there were such a miracle drug, you can be sure that pharmaceutical companies (guess who owns a lot of these companies' stock?) would sell it at an extremely high profit margin, and doctors would use it in a way that would net them big bucks.

Consider, for example, the very few drugs that help people with AIDS. These are priced out of sight, even though they're palliatives and not cures, because AIDS patients are desperate, and will somehow scrape up the money to extend their lives by a few months.

Another problem with the cancer cure legend is that diagnosing cancer requires a series of tests, which are expensive, because there's no single type of cancer. Cancer comes in many forms, and treatment varies with the type.

Yet another aspect of medical treatment is monitoring the patient's condition, which requires more expensive tests and perhaps a period of hospitalization. Again, big bucks, whether the treatment is successful or not.

Finally, we run into side-effects. There's no drug on the market totally without side-effects of some sort. Sometimes, coping with side-effects is a more difficult task than treating the original condition. This offers doctors yet another opportunity to collect high fees.

Now let's look at the alleged miracle drug's effectiveness.[3] Although those who push their "cancer cures" often have testimonials from people allegedly "cured," this isn't evidence. The same goes for other "cures," such as one widely-propagated "cure" for arthritis.[4]

Documenting the effectiveness of any treatment poses several problems in obtaining accurate information. The first problem is accurate diagnosis. It's easy to say that a patient was "cured" of a disease, but essential to establish that he was actually suffering from it at the start. There have been many errors in diagnosis, even among "reputable" doctors, and often a patient will go undiagnosed or misdiagnosed for years while the doctor struggles to "cure" the wrong condition. With cancer, unfortunately, only laboratory tests will provide a sure diagnosis, and even then there's room for error. The bottom line is that some people who've diagnosed themselves as having cancer, or been diagnosed by quacks, never really had it.

Another fudge factor, rarely discussed outside the medical profession, is "spontaneous remission." The human body is a wonderful and still imperfectly-understood mechanism. Even doctors don't fully understand the body's ability to repair itself and sometimes throw off a supposedly "incurable" condition. Cuts and bruises usually heal without medical intervention. Mentally ill people "get over it," and cure themselves. Many "cures" attributed to drugs and other treatments happen because the body often heals itself, sometimes even in spite of the treatment.

Yet another factor is suggestion. The power of suggestion exists, although it's little-understood. The most spectacular effects take place during sessions when subjects are hypnotized to undergo surgery without chemical anesthesia. Some hypnotized subjects can even tolerate being burned, without raising blisters.

Suggestion is little-understood, which is why it's unreliable. However, it's real, and it works for some people. Administering an ineffective drug to a suggestible person can produce a cure, if the person has "faith" and believes what he's told.

Finally, "cancer" is a general term, and covers many conditions quite different from each other. It's actually a catch-all word, and there's no single disease that we can accurately say *is* "cancer." They have different causes, and different prospects of survival. Some are comparatively harmless, while others are the kiss of death. There are even "pre-cancerous conditions," harmless bumps and blisters that may develop into a form of cancer unless removed. No single drug or treatment can possibly "cure" all types.

Identifying Quacks

Let's get one thing straight at the outset. Just as a medical degree or license doesn't automatically mean that a person's qualified to treat patients, lack of an approved license or degree doesn't automatically disqualify someone from providing effective health care. Midwives are legitimate, although obstetricians hate them and lobby against them whenever they can. Some faith-healers manage to attain some cures, although their methods are questionable and unreliable. Chiropractors and osteopaths go through long and intensive training, despite the resentment from the organized medical community.

This is what makes it difficult for you to spot a quack. There's no sure and consistent sign. There are, however, some warning symptoms, forms of behavior that alert you to be careful:

◆ One is the claim that the drug has a "secret" ingredient. No legitimate drug is secret, because it's necessary to reveal its composition to the U.S. Food and Drug Administration. Keeping a drug secret has only one real effect, as far as you're concerned. It prevents an outside party from evaluating it. If you find this hard to believe, look at cosmetics. Cosmetic manufacturers advertise "secret" formulas with ingredients identified only by initials, numbers, or cryptic and meaningless names. They make all sorts of claims for these secret ingredients, and cosmetics continue to sell well, despite their being composed mainly of various oils, perfumes, and fatty substances. The profit mark-up is high, and the main reason for the secrecy is to prevent the customer from knowing that the ingredients are available at a price far less than that of the "secret" formula.

◆ Promising a quick and painless cure is another deception. Unfortunately, many legitimate cures for serious conditions are neither quick nor painless. However, to someone who needs to believe that he has a chance of survival without rigorous treatment, the promise of a quick and painless cure has an overpowering appeal.

◆ Watch out for "treatments" for fictitious disorders. There's no such thing as "cellulite," and dandruff is normal shedding of scalp cells. Yet we find books and "treatments" attracting dollars from suckers.

◆ Similarly, body odor is not a disorder. Sweat is a normal product of sweat glands in the skin. A shower a day takes care of personal cleanliness in all but the hottest climates. Yet many Americans buy harsh chemicals sold as "deodorants," and apply them to their skins. Some of these chemicals cause irritations, and become medical problems.

◆ Also, watch out for new and radical diets. Weight loss is a problem for many Americans, and new diet books appear every year, some even written by doctors. However inspirational the book may be, hardly any diets work, and this fuels the desperate demand for new systems each year.

◆ Testimonials are an especially blatant and misleading form of advertising, and regularly appear in ads. Testimonials are usually signed in a way that makes it impossible for the reader to verify, such as "J.S., Kansas City." Even a live testimonial by someone you know is chancy. Although he may claim to feel better, this doesn't prove he was ever cured, or that the cure was the result of the alleged remedy. The "cure" may be only a temporary respite, with a relapse on the way.

◆ Don't be fooled by an impressive degree attributed to the person who supposedly invented the "cure" being advertised. Some degrees are totally fake, and others are legitimate, but the ad doesn't tell you anything you really need to know about the inventor's background. For example, a certain "Doctor" Carey Reams has been convicted of practicing medicine without a license in four states.[5]

◆ Beware of any health-related product that promises any sort of "guarantee." Legitimate doctors don't guarantee their work, for the best of reasons. Any guarantee would open them up to lawsuits for malpractice, because often they just can't cure their patients! Some quack "cures" use the guarantee as part of the rip-off.[6]

◆ Watch out for any strange and unconventional "diagnostic tests." It's impossible to diagnose cancer from saliva, for example, although many people don't know this. Also watch out for any devices with colored lights. The big problem here is that many of these fraudulent "diagnostic" and "therapeutic" devices are made to resemble legitimate electro-mechanical apparatus used by real doctors and laboratory technicians. Anyone unfamiliar with medical electronics would find it hard to distinguish between a CAT scanner and a quack device such as an "orgone box," for example.

◆ Another tip-off is a claim of exotic ingredients, such as Oriental seaweed. This, too, is hard to evaluate, unless you have a very good bio-medical background. Many legitimate drugs come from unusual sources. Penicillin is found in bread mold, and rauwolfia comes from a South American plant. If you don't know for sure, check it out.

◆ The most common areas for health quackery are arthritis cures, weight-loss programs, pills, or diets, hair growth, rejuvenation treatments, and impotence cures. Take a good look at any such claims before buying, because historically they've been the most lucrative areas for sharp operators.

Protecting Yourself

The first step is to be informed. Information on quackery is easy to find with little effort, as there are several information sources listed in the "resources" chapter at the end of this book.

Secondly, be very skeptical of unorthodox treatments. The medical establishment is bad enough, with its greed-directed policies and treatments. Unfortunately, unconventional practitioners, however sincere they may be, very poor at establishing scientifically that their treatments have any benefit at all.

Notes:

1. *The Arizona Republic*, November 12, 1985.
2. *Age Page*, U.S. Department of Health and Human Services, Public Health Service, August, 1985.
3. *Ibid.,* Some of these treatments consist of low-protein diets or apparently worthless drugs, such as Laetrile.
4. *Frauds Against the Elderly*, Select Committee on Aging, House of Representatives, Ninety-seventh Congress, May 20, 1981. Boston, p. 4. Other frauds are "vision diets." pp. 8-9.
5. *Frauds Against the Elderly*, p. 39. A fascinating account of how this health fraud artist worked on an investigator posing as a "patient" is in the affidavit of Richard Paul, pp. 97-100. Another account is the affidavit of Mary Pasciucco, also an investigator, pp. 100-101. Both described in great detail how they were "tested" and "treated" for conditions such as: "Notable adrenal stress, demineralization, osteroarthritic changes, delata cells in colon, notable inward tension-tiredness, bruises too easily, heals too slowly, liver function depressed, sugar fluctuates, in the zone for a minor heart attack, mineral and oxygen transport poor, stress on the right kidney, stress on the bladder, and stress around the ileocecal valve region."
6. A diet pill ad on a national cable-TV channel was of this type. The ad promised quick weight loss with the pills and while following the program. The price of the first package of pills was $19.95. These pills sold in a local drugstore for about three dollars. The "guarantee" offered was that, if the first package of pills didn't produce the expected weight loss, the customer would get a second package "free" for $2.95 "shipping and handling." The ingenuity of this scheme is admirable. The customer would pay an

inflated price for the first shipment, and normal retail price for subsequent ones, as long as he continued to be taken in.

Chapter 12
Psychologists And
Other Headshrinkers

In the "good old days," people with emotional problems used to consult older and wiser family members, clergymen, and society's elders. These people didn't have the aura of being scientific, but they provided dedicated care. Today, many people automatically think of a headshrinker when they face problems.

Behavioral science is the youngest of the sciences, so undeveloped that it's not really a science in the same way as other fields. Its stage of development is like that of medicine in the nineteenth century, overlaid with legend and superstition. Because behavioral science deals with intangibles, it's hard to pin down, and this leaves the field wide open to charlatanism.

We can easily measure a person's height or weight, using simple tools with definite and well-known margins of error. Similarly, we can measure a person's temperature, blood pressure, and other physical signs. Sophisticated laboratory tests can pin down blood type, sugar level, brainwave patterns, and other workings of the body.

Measuring the workings of the mind is different. We find many theories, but few facts. Psychology is more like religion than like science. Let's skim the surface of this field, to get a historical perspective. We'll just sketch the highlights in this chapter, because this is a very complicated subject, and truly most of it isn't worth noting. One traditional folk belief about psychiatrists and psychoanalysts is that "they're crazier than their patients." While this sounds like redneck, cracker-barrel philosophy, something only an uneducated person would say, there's more truth to it than is at first apparent. For example, psychiatrists have one of the highest suicide rates among occupational groups. A close look at some of the specific fields shows up some glaring faults, and serious failings among the practitioners and their methods.

Freud and Psychoanalysis

Sigmund Freud was a nineteenth-century neurologist, addicted to cocaine, who became interested in the workings of the human personality. He was a moody, introspective man who had many fantasies, and observed that other people had fantasies as well. He made the mistake of thinking that his fantasies applied to other people, and this was the foundation of "psychoanalysis," and the Freudian theories of personality.

From the start, psychoanalysis had many of the features of religious sects. Freud's early followers didn't see eye to eye with him, nor with each other. Carl Jung, while agreeing with Freud's basic premise of the "unconscious mind" determining personality, emphasized different aspects of development. Carl Jung set up his own "school" of psychoanalysis, as did Alfred Adler and other disciples. Wilhelm Reich, for example, had different ideas which included the "orgone," a particle that affects well-being, and he set up his own following. Other psychoanalytic schools have been named after their founders, such as Horney, Reik, White, etc.

All schools agree on the importance of early childhood experiences in shaping personality. This, however, isn't a profound insight because it goes along with common experiences, and even folk knowledge. The old proverb, "As the twig is bent, the tree shall grow," expressed it long before Freud and his followers appeared on the scene. However, psychoanalysts went off the deep end, ascribing strange complexes to their patients. Basically, they were "projecting" their fantasies upon their patients in a way that amounted to intellectual blackjacking, and left patients no choice but to accept them.

The technique of "psychoanalysis" is simple. The patient "free associates," saying anything that comes to mind, and the psychoanalyst offers his "interpretations" of these thoughts. He may tell his patient that his problem arises from a wish to have sex with his mother, an early hatred of his father, etc.

If the patient disagrees, the psychoanalyst doesn't re-think or re-evaluate his theory. He simply tells his patient that he's showing "resistance," or that he doesn't have the proper insight into his own mind. If the patient denies having any such thoughts or memories, the psychoanalyst states that he's "blocking" them from consciousness, and that they're really there, buried in his subconscious. Freud outlined the technique in these words: "We must not be led astray by initial denials. If we keep firmly to what we have inferred, we shall in the end conquer every resistance by emphasizing the unshakable nature of our convictions."[1]

This is intellectual blackjacking at its worst, and is a no-win situation for the patient. He has to take the psychoanalyst's word for everything, because by becoming his patient, he's surrendered the right to his own opinion. He's admitted mental incompetence, and placed himself in the hands of someone who claims superior knowledge.

Over-generalization is their standard method of operation. If one patient reports a dream, psychoanalysts treat it as typical of others who have similar complaints, and formulate a theory from it. Reading psychoanalytic literature discloses that most of them report on one patient at a time, weaving complex theories based on the results with that individual.

This is what accounts for many of the bizarre theories put forth by psychoanalysts. They over-generalize, attributing their conclusions in one case to people as a whole. Freud, for example, dealt mainly with nineteenth century Viennese people who were affluent enough to afford his fees, and his statements on human behavior are valid only for this small group. This is why his theories are top-heavy with sexual repression and hysterical manifestations relating to Victorian sexual morality. The working-class people of the era were not sexually inhibited as were the affluent strivers, and didn't develop these hangups. Nor did the very rich, who had very loose codes of sexual conduct. People in other countries had their own problems, which bore little relation to those of the middle-class Viennese.[2]

One characteristic of quackery is jargon, using complex and abstruse language to describe ordinary things and events. More than most medical professionals, psychoanalysts are prone to using jargon. Their writings are filled with terms such as "catharsis," "cathexis," "introjection," "retrojection," etc. This helps to keep outsiders in the dark, and dresses up guesswork in the guise of scientific knowledge. The term, "psychobabble," has emerged to denote psychological/psychiatric jargon, although, ironically, the coiner of the term, R.D. Rosen, is a believer in Freudian psychoanalysis.

One outstanding feature of psychoanalytic treatment is the time it takes, and the amount of money needed to pay for three to five sessions per week for several years. Neurosis is the rich person's hobby, if the "treatment" is psychoanalysis. The analyst is in the driver's seat, because he can keep the patient going as long as his money and credulity last. Although the patient may say that he feels better, this doesn't let him off the hook. Analysts call this "remission of symptoms," an effort to drop the symptoms in order to avoid revealing unconscious thoughts the patient would rather not face. The analyst tells his patient that he still has "unconscious conflicts" to resolve, and that this will require more therapy. This usually works, because after all, the doctor is the expert, and he fosters a remunerative dependency relationship with his patient.

Sometimes, outright venality shapes the relationship. The Kansas City therapist who sold one of his patients five houses, four cars, and two boats during a 17-year therapy marathon was obviously exploiting the relationship to do a little business on the side.[3]

Dr. Frederick A. Goodwin, Director of the National Institute of Mental Health, states that the prospects of the Clinton Health Plan covering psychoanalysis are bleak. The reason he gives is that "there's no real evidence that it works."[4]

Does it Work?

The average "cure" rate reported by psychoanalysts is about 50 percent.[5] Even this figure is questionable because it comes only from psychoanalysts' own evaluations of their cases and successes. There's no objective evidence to support even this modest figure. What makes this worse is the extremely defensive attitudes of psychoanalysts. Their course of "training" is long and extensive, and includes a "training analysis," during which the future analyst is himself psychoanalyzed. Psychoanalysts claim that anyone who has not been through it is not in a position to evaluate it properly.[6] This is very much like the self-protective attitudes displayed by doctors and police officers, who insist that anyone outside the brotherhood lacks the knowledge to understand the issues and problems involved, and therefore cannot judge them. In other words, they can only judge themselves, and the rest of us have to take their word for it that they're doing a good job.

How do they judge themselves and evaluate their work? The same way in which they produce their theories, that's how! Typically, they over-generalize on the basis of one patient.[7] This is the process they dress up in impressive-sounding language, calling it "clinical experience."

Psychoanalysts and psychotherapists resent efforts to measure the effectiveness of their work, maintaining that "individual clinical judgment" is the only valid standard (in other words, take their word for it) and that quantification results in over-simplification.[8]

Shrinks always have explanations, excuses, and rationalizations when their efforts result in disaster. The suicide of a Boston psychiatrist's patient was not terribly unusual, although it did raise some questions.

A landmark lawsuit was "Osheroff vs. Chestnut Lodge," which resulted after a 42-year-old medical doctor, suffering from depression, signed himself into Chestnut Lodge, a private psychiatric hospital. There, he received psychotherapy for seven months, which produced no improvement. His condition actually deteriorated, and he transferred himself to another hospital, where he received drug therapy. This produced enough improvement so that he was discharged within three months. However, the prolonged hospitalization had resulted in the loss of his practice and the custody of his children. He sued, claiming that Chestnut Lodge had been negligent, and won an out-of-court settlement after an arbitration panel found in his favor.[9]

Osheroff was one unusual case in which the victim was sophisticated enough, and had enough connections, to obtain satisfaction through the legal process. There has been no study of how many patients have been victimized by uncaring or incompetent psychiatrists, but have been too deteriorated or too ignorant to sue. Many languish on back, in the custody of family members, or on the street, after having had their brains fried or sliced by avid shockiatrists or psychosurgeons. The ugly fact is that heavy application of brain-damaging treatments can make a patient a vegetable, too apathetic and too confused to testify against a shrink.

Psychotherapies, Counseling, and Other Treatments

Are other forms of therapy any more effective? There are many other forms of "psychotherapy" and "counseling," and many of the same problems exist with them. Many are based on Freudian and other forms of analysis, and depend solely on the "therapist's" judgment.

Psychiatry has also seen physical methods of therapy, such as electro-shock and lobotomy. When introduced during the late 1930s and early 1940s, these treatments came into wide use in state hospitals. State hospitals were typically over-crowded in those days, with a patient/doctor ratio of 100 to one and even as high as 800 to one in some chronic wards. This didn't allow for time-consuming diagnosis or therapy, only for mass production.

This was the stone age of psychiatry. An "intake interview," during which the psychiatrist had to arrive at a diagnosis and formulate a "treatment plan," took as little as five minutes. "Treatment" was quick and dirty. The electro-shock scene in the film *One Flew Over the Cuckoo's Nest* is a realistic portrayal of the brutal methods of the era. It's also accurate, as shown in the film, that electro-shock was often used as punishment instead of therapy.

Psychiatrists, as eager to experiment and get published as any other doctors, applied electro-shock and lobotomy to all sorts of patients. ECT (electro-convulsive therapy) was used for a variety of "disorders," including schizophrenia, manic-depressive psychosis, neurosis, homosexuality, anxiety, tics, Tourette's Syndrome, psychopathic personality, and even to reduce pain in terminal cancer patients.[10]

Pre-frontal lobotomy and other techniques of "psychosurgery" had equally bizarre applications.[11] Lobotomists were convinced that brain surgery, or a refinement thereof, would help a large variety of psychiatric patients, and some diagnostic categories that weren't even in the book. They used lobotomy and its variants (topectomy, thalamectomy, transorbital lobotomy, etc.) for psychosis, psychopathic personality, anxiety, manic attacks, and again to cope with terminal cancer pain.[12]

These widespread and indiscriminate applications at first seemed to bring great success. After all, if a psychiatrist introduced a new "treatment," used it on 100 patients, and proclaimed that it had helped most of them, his word was accepted. Both the professional literature and popular magazines were filled with stories of quick and remarkable "cures."

This couldn't last, for two important reasons. The first was the severe side-effects of these "treatments." ECT produced convulsions, often resulting in broken bones and other injuries, and a death rate of between one and four percent, depending on the time and place of the study.

Pre-frontal lobotomy and its variants also had a death rate, again varying with the time and place. The "open" lobotomies, in which the surgeon opened the skull to cut the nerve fibers, had a death rate averaging about one percent. In a "closed" operation, the surgeon would drill a hole at each temple and insert a "leucotome" (an instrument shaped like a flattened ice-pick, but with two sharp edges) to cut the nerve fibers targeted for destruction, the risk was higher because the surgeon worked blind, unable to see blood vessels. A fatal hemorrhage could result from severing a blood vessel.

Most dangerous was the "transorbital" lobotomy, in which the surgeon slipped the leucotome under each eye-lid and hammered it through the bone into the brain. When the surgeon swung the leucotome in an arc to sever nerve fibers, any blood vessels in the way also got cut, and the death rate averaged about four percent. However, the transorbital operation was the quickest to perform, often taking no longer than an infant circumcision.

In some cases, the surgeon didn't even use conventional anesthesia, instead knocking the patient out with a jolt of ECT, and inserting the leucotome during the several minutes of unconsciousness that followed.

Brain surgery produced immediate and profound personality changes, often more detrimental than the illness itself. One thing quickly became clear about lobotomy — it did not "cure" at all. Instead, it merely reduced the severity of the symptoms. A patient with ideas of persecution, who assaulted everyone he met, would retain his delusions after surgery, but would be much calmer. Cutting the nerve pathways reduced the intensity of his emotions. A parallel effect was that the patient would also lose much of his normal drive. Yet another after-effect was weight gain, because lobotomized patients slowed down.

Psychosurgery often acted as a powerful and permanent sedative, and the amount of brain tissue destroyed determined the amount of sedation. In many instances, the patient would end up so profoundly sedated that psychiatrists would describe him as a "vegetable." It quickly became clear that lobotomy was the most drastic and irreversible treatment, for use only if symptoms were intolerable and unmanageable, and after everything else had failed.

This made lobotomy a favorite in state mental hospitals, where the patient load was so heavy that in many instances only custodial care was possible. A ward full of violent patients could be calmed dramatically by slicing their frontal lobes, which made custodial care much easier because it required a smaller staff. State hospital administrators viewed psychosurgery as an important custodial care measure for "incurable" cases. Later, tranquilizers produced a profound calming effect without the need for surgery, and lobotomy went into decline.

Lobotomy was rarely used for private patients, because the brain damage was so severe that the patient was never his old self again. The dividing line was a choice between the lesser of two evils — the symptoms and the side-effects of the surgery. Only when there was no other choice would psychiatrists consider lobotomy for private patients, and only after other treatments, such as ECT, had failed.

The second reason for the decline in the use of these treatments was that they rarely worked. This became obvious immediately with lobotomized patients, and lobotomy was never used as the treatment of choice after the enthusiasm of the first few years. However, the first few years were filled with abuses, such as operating on children as young as four.

ECT, because it produced fewer immediate and dramatic side-effects, remained in use. Its application spread, and some psychiatrists, such as Bellevue Hospital's Dr. Lauretta Bender, used it on children as young as three. In the long run, it became apparent that there were unanswered questions about the "success" rate, and the reason that these questions remained unanswered was that nobody had asked them for a surprisingly long time.

With any disorder, physical or mental, there is a phenomenon known as "spontaneous remission." The patient recovers, with or without treatment. We see this most readily in the case of a common cold, because there's no known cure and the cold disappears after about a week. It's less easy to determine in the case of mental problems, because they're intangible. However, common experience tells us that many people go through periods of depression, often brought on by real-life events, and they get over them sooner or later. It works the same way for other problems. A proportion of patients get better whatever the treatment, or even with no treatment at all.[13]

Conscientious psychiatrists came to realize that a "study" of, say, 100 patients given ECT was useless without a "control group." This meant a similar group of patients with the same diagnosis, who received only custodial care while the treatment group got ECT. It would then be possible to measure the effectiveness of the treatment by comparing the two groups' recovery rates. During the 1950s, many such studies took place, covering all sorts of physical treatment, psychoanalysis, and psychotherapy. The results were uniform and disappointing. None of these forms of treatment, when properly compared, showed any significant curative effect.

The evidence was massive and, therefore, overwhelming. Generally, mental patients divided up into three groups. About one-third would recover completely, one-third would show some improvement, and the last third would show no improvement at all. These ratios held true despite the "treatment" studied.

The fact of spontaneous remission had led to a serious misapprehension among psychiatrists. It had long been believed that prompt treatment, whatever the method, would produce the best results. Gradually, the reason for this became clear. Patients who were going to recover would do so within the first few months after the onset of symptoms. Any treatment used during those first few months would make no difference at all, but it would appear that the treatment had caused the recovery. Treatment applied after this initial period would encompass only those much less likely to recover, and have a much lower rate of "success."

Other research has also shown that patients with simpler and less overwhelming problems tend to benefit more quickly from "therapy."[14] Another study, focusing on depressed patients, found that "patients who were less severely depressed at entry got better on any treatment..."[15] The conclusion that simpler problems are easier to solve isn't exactly a profound insight, but it's typical of the way psycho-shrinks present an obvious fact as the result of monumental research.

Many psychiatrists, nevertheless, ignored these findings, and continued using ECT. One reason was simply empirical. Although there was no scientific validity, they claimed that the treatments worked for them in their experience with their patients. Another reason was the ease with which a psychiatrist could apply ECT. The method could be used on out-patients, and some of these "shockiatrists" used ECT during office visits. At the time, the going rate for ECT was about fifty dollars per treatment, the same as a psychiatrist would charge for an hour's psychotherapy. Administering several ECT treatments in one hour allowed collecting several fees because the treatment itself took only a few minutes, and the patient spent the rest of the hour sleeping it off. This was far more time-saving and remunerative than listening to a patient speaking about his problems for an hour, and the method lent itself to mass production.

Lee Atwater, well-known American political figure of the 1980s, once characterized receiving electro-shock treatments as "being hooked up to jumper cables." He wasn't exaggerating by much.

Dishonest Research

Psychiatry, and medicine in general, are full of discarded therapies that first appeared promising, but later proved ineffective. Yet, dishonest tactics effectively promoted their use. An example is the psychiatrist pushing ECT for depression. He selects as patients only people depressed because of the recent death of a relative. Almost all make "miraculous" recoveries after a few shock treatments, which results in a successful article in a medical publication.

The influence of dishonest researchers out to make names for themselves affected both professional and public perceptions of these treatments. In psychiatry, as in any other curative field, there are certain factors that affect the outcome, or prognosis:

1. *Age.* The younger the patient is, the more resilient, and the more likely he is to recover, whatever the disorder.
2. *Onset.* An emotional problem that suddenly occurred is easier to treat than one that's been building for a long time.
3. *Duration of illness.* The longer a person's been ill, the less likely the recovery.
4. *State of health before present illness.* A person generally in good health and well-adjusted has a much better chance of recovery than one who's been in poor shape even before the current problem.

It's very easy for a dishonest researcher to stack the deck in his selection of patients for a new treatment. Choosing young, previously healthy patients ill for only a short time will always produce high "recovery" rates. On the other hand, selecting very deteriorated patients from the chronic ward will produce a cure rate of almost zero every time.

The researcher hyping a new treatment to attain recognition in his field need only choose his patients carefully. Once he's published, he can protect his reputation for a long time even after other psychiatrists find that his new treatment doesn't work as well as originally claimed. He need only state that others did not apply the treatment in the same way, therefore compromising its effectiveness. This also subtly suggests that his challengers are not as skilled as he.

Drugs

The coming of mood-altering and anti-psychotic drugs also led to the decline of radical psychiatric "treatments." Drugs lend themselves well to controlled studies by several means. The most valid is to divide patients into three groups. One receives the drug under test. The second receives placebos, pills with inert ingredients. The third receives nothing at all. Comparing the recovery rates between the three groups shows how many recoveries are due to the drug, how many due to the effect of suggestion, and how many result from spontaneous remission.

One study of the effects of psychotherapy and drugs used four groups of depressed patients, two receiving different kinds of psycho-therapies, one group receiving an antidepressant drug (imipramine) and the fourth a placebo. The most striking result was that "those on the antidepressant drug recovered more quickly and more effectively."[16] This study was typical of recent well-controlled research.

With overwhelming evidence that only psychoactive drugs have shown any effectiveness, why do psychiatrists continue to use questionable and ineffective methods such as psychotherapy and ECT? Greed is only part of the answer. The other part is a fantastic complex of rationalizations to support their use. The term "supportive therapy" leads to many abuses. The main idea is to support the patient emotionally while the drug, the real treatment, is working. "Supportive therapy" is admittedly ineffective in attaining the cure, but it offers an opportunity for the psychiatrist to collect more in fees than he would if he simply wrote a prescription. It's also defensive medicine. Having the patient come in once a week gives the psychiatrist the opportunity to monitor his progress and note any side-effects. This can be important in court, if a malpractice suit results.

Psychiatrists also believe in what they're doing. We can see this by reading the articles in their professional journals. Sometimes they describe a treatment's failure, but not in terms that blame the treatment or the psychiatrist's judgment in selecting a particular treatment.

More than conventional medicos, psychiatrists are prone to using weaseling phrases such as "the patient failed to respond to therapy." It's not necessary to read between the lines to get this. It's there in black-and-white. The psychiatrist never describes a failure as his fault. You don't see phrases such as "I prescribed the wrong treatment," or "I made an error is judgment." It's always the patient's fault.

The Thirty-Day Clinic

Psychiatry is profitable, and has become more so with the increased willingness of insurance plans to pay benefits for psychiatric care. The number of for-profit psychiatric hospitals in this country was 21,400 in 1984; by 1990, it had grown to 37,500. What was startling was the number of clinics offering plans expressly tailored to take advantage of the benefits laid out by the insurers, as we'll see.

Psychological "counseling" services today are being advertised and packaged by professional marketers who tailor the product or service to current economic conditions. Newspaper advertisements for alcoholism recovery centers, adolescent treatment centers, and other in-patient and out-patient services usually offer a 30-day plan. This is because most medical insurance payment schedules limit treatment to 30 days, and marketers tailor their packages to what insurance providers will pay.

A congressional investigation in 1992 revealed that private psychiatric hospitals had imprisoned thousands of "adolescents, children, and adults for psychiatric treatments they didn't need." Some hospitals even employed bounty hunters to procure people with mental health insurance, and these "patients were confined until benefits ran out."[17]

What's happened is the "medicalization" of normal and natural conditions. If your son is finding school difficult, he has, according to these people, a treatable "learning disorder," and you ought to sign him into their in-patient clinic for their 30-day special program. Such clinics publish shotgun lists of "symptoms" that they hope you'll interpret as requiring treatment. Symptom lists include moodiness, loss of appetite, change in sleeping habits, crying, spending a lot of time alone, disobedience, and other behaviors normally found in adolescence. To clinic operators, though, these are symptoms of possible drug abuse, depression, and other conditions calling for their 30-day cure. Adolescents who escape this sort of "treatment" have far more interesting hazards waiting for them when they grow up.

The Sex Therapy Mess

As old diseases and disorders are cured or vanish, new ones take their place, to keep therapists fully employed. When necessary, these therapists will invent disorders so that they can "cure" them. Psychological mythology thrives in such an environment.

One myth is that of the simultaneous orgasm. Generations of psychoanalysts and other shrinks have gotten lots of mileage from this one, which has justified countless hours of "therapy" and, of course, incalculable sums of money. The notion that ideal sex necessarily involves perfectly synchronized climaxes between partners is an unattainable ideal for many, who are made to feel inadequate.

Thus the sex therapist. Sex therapists can be moderate practitioners, who merely advise on sexual technique and prescribe exercises to cure "premature ejaculation," or they may be "sexual surrogates" who actually perform sex acts with their clients. Sex for pay is an age-old profession. The dividing line between a full-contact sex therapist and a prostitute is practically non-existent.

There is fierce and continual jockeying for clients, and theories follow suit. Shrinks maintained for years that any male who did not hold back his orgasm until his partner caught up had a psychological problem, probably based on deep-seated hostility towards women. Today, the new psychology maintains that it's merely a lack of training, and that sex therapists can provide the proper training.

Likewise for impotence, which shrinks held was the result of "performance anxiety," hostility, and other strictly mental causes. This theory didn't hold up, and now male impotence is once more in the hands of medical doctors, who have found physical causes treatable by drugs, exercises, and even surgery.

The Psychiatrist in Court

Perhaps the most glaring example of greed among psychiatrists occurs when they testify as "expert witnesses" in court. The reason lawyers call upon psychiatrists is because the "Not guilty by reason of insanity" (NGRI) defense has been with us since the "M'Naughten Rule" of 1844. This rule, devised by a British court, stated that a person was not guilty if he did not know the nature or consequences of his actions. During the early part of this century, the "Durham Rule" came about in America, and this modified and eased the requirement for a successful "NGRI" defense. Under the Durham Rule, the verdict is "not guilty" if the criminal act is "the product of mental disorder." This opened the door to widespread abuses, because all a defense lawyer now needed was an expert witness to testify that his client was suffering from a "mental disorder" which caused him to break the law.

The John Hinckley trial was a significant example of this tactic during recent history. Hinckley was accused of shooting U.S. President Ronald Reagan and three others, and his guilt was plain because of videotapes and eyewitness testimony. Hinckley's attorney used the NGRI defense. The prosecution felt otherwise, maintaining that Hinckley was sane enough to know what he was doing.

Thus we saw the spectacle of two teams of four psychiatrists each, one working for the prosecution and the other for the defense, offering contradictory opinions. Those for the prosecution said that Hinckley was sane. Those for the defense argued he wasn't. The outcome isn't the important point here, and neither is Hinckley's guilt or innocence. What's significant is that each team of psychiatrists tailored its testimony to suit the needs of the party paying its fees. This leads to the topic of "opinions for hire."

"Expert witnesses" often deal with tangible evidence, such as fingerprints or blood types, and their testimonies are verifiable by laboratory examination. Psychiatrists, on the other hand, deal with intangibles, and this offers a fertile field for both honest differences of opinion and chicanery. The situation's made worse by the sort of issues involved. A defendant who is obviously insane, so severely "out of it" that even the judge, jury, and audience can see it immediately, doesn't need a psychiatrist speaking for him. The prosecution, on the other hand, will be wondering if the defendant is faking it, and may hire a psychiatrist to uncover the truth if possible. The defense attorney will hire his own to support his case.

This is why we've seen such imaginative absurdities as the "battered woman" syndrome, a new "diagnosis" made up to justify the killing or wounding of a mate by his wife. The theory, as presented by psychological experts for hire, is that an abused woman becomes so deranged that she is justified in killing or mutilating her husband, even long after the abuse that allegedly caused the "disorder" is over. This is how Lorena Bobbitt, who cut off her husband's penis, got away with an "insanity" verdict.

Expert psychiatric witnesses appear in civil suits, as well. When former GTE employees sued the company's New Mexico branch for damages resulting from exposure to toxic chemicals, GTE employed Elissa Benedek, a psychiatrist who had been President of the American Psychiatric Association in 1991, to testify on its behalf so as to discredit the employees' claims. Dr. Benedek stated that workers had problems such as "chronic unhappiness."[18]

Lawyers know very well that there are "opinions for hire." There is a corps of professional "expert witnesses" who earn their livings by testifying according to the needs of their clients. This leads to the hiring and lining up of contradictory expert witnesses in a trial. Usually, the effect is to confuse the issues, and make a true verdict harder to attain.

Intelligence

What is intelligence, and how is it measured? Nobody can provide a definitive answer to those questions. The best practical answer is that "intelligence is what is measured by intelligence tests."

Wracked by controversy, the field of intelligence testing is too uncertain to be called "science." A few of the highlights are:

The same person will attain different scores on different tests. The same person will attain different scores on the same test at different times. This is like measuring a window with tape measures made by different companies, and arriving at a different measurement with each one.

There is no clear correlation between high scores on I.Q. tests and personal wealth. People who score highly do not necessarily become rich. Some people who score modestly gain great wealth, because of great drive and perhaps a lack of scruples.

There is a difference in average scores between races. In the United States, Blacks generally score somewhat lower than Whites. This result, confirmed by testing many thousand people of both races, had psychologists tap-dancing around their tests, trying to maintain that the tests are valid while repudiating the "politically incorrect" findings that not all men are created equal. Some "PC" psychologists explained this away by stating that intelligence tests are "culturally biased" against non-Whites. However, this doesn't explain how Japanese attained higher scores than Americans on the same test.

There is a high-IQ society, Mensa, founded by a British psychologist, Sir Cyril Burt, in 1945. As of this writing, the American branch has about 55,000 members. The requirement for membership is to score in the top two percent of the distribution curve of an intelligence test. The exact score varies with the test, but more significantly, IQ tests aren't accurate or reliable enough to measure so precisely. The test-taker's physical and mental state, including factors such as hunger, fatigue, and general mood, can lead to very different scores on the same test.

Burt, Mensa's founder, established a reputation as a researcher in human intelligence. However, after his death he was accused of falsifying "more than three decades of data, from the mid 1940s to 1966," to back up his theory on the relationship between heredity and intelligence.[19]

The Media Shrinks

Newspapers, magazines, and TV are laced with columns by psychologists and psychiatrists, and some of these shrinks make guest appearances whenever there's a sensational news item with psychiatric aspects. An example is when there's a sensational mass murder, such as the "McDonald's Massacre" during the middle 1980s. Every TV network had its expert shrink, none of whom had ever met James Huberty, to present his opinion of what was in the killer's mind. Likewise, when the Jeffrey Dahmer case was in the headlines, media shrinks appeared to pontificate on Dahmer's mental state.

Media shrinks appear on regular news programs, network news "specials," and of course, talk shows. Some appear for fees, while others take advantage of the opportunity to gain some exposure. None of the newscasters ever says anything to challenge their guests' credibility, of course. Nobody brings up the questions: "Since you've never met Smith, how do you know what he was thinking?" "How can you make a diagnosis of a person you've never examined?"

The danger in this is that viewers will not take it as merely entertainment, but as a demonstration that a suitable "expert" can make a remote-control psychiatric diagnosis of an individual he's never met.

Predicting Workplace Honesty

Since pre-employment testing by polygraph (the notorious "lie detector," long discredited) was outlawed in most occupations several years ago, the focus has been on pencil-and-paper tests. Several companies specializing in devising these tests as predictors of employee honesty and other personality traits have advertised their wares in specialist magazines such as *Security Management*. However, there have been serious challenges to these tests, some as a result of U.S. Government studies. Agencies such as the Office of Technology Assessment reported serious doubts regarding the validity of these tests.

Even members of the security industry found faults. Brian C. Jayne, Director of research and development for John E. Reid and Associates, Inc., a major provider of tests, admitted in an article for fellow security professionals that these tests have their problems. In a study conducted by Reid and Associates of individuals who took their tests and were later suspects in workplace incidents, real-life results did not accord well with predictions based on these tests. Of 59 people who failed the tests, only 44 percent turned out to be guilty. Jayne concluded that an applicant's attitude about honesty, as measured by the tests, was not a reliable guide to future behavior.[20]

What he concluded *was* a reliable guide, past behavior, is more expensive to check, which is one reason test-producers are so successful in selling their short-cuts. A background check is more time-consuming, and more expensive, than a quick and dirty test.

Zany Sidelights of Psychological Therapy

A currently fashionable sub-specialty of psychotherapy is digging out "repressed memories" involving sexual abuse from years or decades before. Some therapists bully their patients into thinking that the root cause of their problems are long-repressed memories, and what emerges is limited only by the therapist's fantasies. This trend has reached "epidemic" proportions, according to Paul McHugh, a psychiatrist who is chairman of the psychiatry department at Johns Hopkins University.[21]

One woman was pressured by her therapist into fabricating false memories of rape by her father during childhood. The especially dangerous aspect of this sort of psychological fantasy is that the accused has absolutely no defense. Denials by the perpetrator are expected and summarily discounted. Nobody expects supporting physical evidence, such as semen and blood stains, to remain years after the event. It's also impossible to produce alibis for events alleged to have taken place so long ago.

One reason for this trendy malpractice is that there is big money if a lawsuit develops. An "abused" daughter can sue a wealthy father for damages, with the lawyer and the psychologist who testifies as an "expert witness" getting their cuts.

The main reason patients conform to the therapist's fantasies is in the nature of the relationship between therapist and patient. The patient sees the therapist as someone trying to help him, places his trust in the therapist, and accepts the therapist's authority. Some patients go so far as to make up memories to please their therapists.

An even zanier aspect of repressed memories coming to the surface is the patient who "recalls" being abducted by aliens from outer space.[22] When organized religion was in vogue, some hysterical people reported "visions" of a religious nature, such as seeing angels or even the Virgin Mary. Today, space aliens are more trendy, and these take the place of religious figures for kooks. Of course, therapists are perfectly happy to run with whatever ball fate hands them, as long as there's money to make.

Another form of false-memory syndrome is the recalling of satanic rituals and abuses inflicted on patients. This, too, is a result of "satanism" being a trendy topic today, further sensationalized by the yellow press and tabloid TV. Patients report child and animal sacrifices in such profusion that there should be bodies turning up almost everywhere, but the notable feature of these satanic "memories" is that no physical evidence turns up to support them.

Protecting Yourself

What can you do to avoid the hazards and abuses of freewheeling shrinks? The most obvious defense is not to succumb to mental problems, but for some people this is impossible. If you're one of the unlucky ones who has a problem he can't handle, there are defensive measures available to you, both to protect your mind and body, and to avoid economic rape.

If you have an emotional problem you can't handle, seek help as soon as possible. More important is the decision to seek the right sort of help. If you're religious, go to your clergyman. Most are fairly sophisticated, and can be quite helpful. They usually have lots of experience in counseling parishioners. Most importantly, they're doing it for humanitarian reasons, not because they're chasing the buck.

If a clergyman isn't the choice for you, talk your problems over with a close friend or family member in whom you have confidence. This is more important than it might seem at first, because people with close family ties and close friends are less likely to be overwhelmed by crushing problems that wreck their mental stability. Emotional support is intangible, but real, especially when it comes from an understanding friend or relative, and not from a psychiatrist trying to milk you for every dollar he can.

Remember that often, simply "talking it out" with someone does a lot of good. Getting it off your chest will often bring a sense of relief, especially if the person with whom you're discussing your problem has had a similar one himself. One great barrier people with problems face is that they think their problems are unique, that nobody else ever faced a similar experience, or can understand the way they feel. It's very helpful to find others who have had the same experiences, and because of that can understand the situation. The success of non-professional support groups such as Alcoholics Anonymous shows this well.

If your problem is so severe that you can't function, and the people you seek out to help you say that you need professional help, be especially careful. Contrary to the popular stereotype, people with severe and incapacitating emotional problems are not totally "crazy" and unable to help themselves or understand what's happening around them. Very few psychotics are so out of it that they're completely helpless and at the mercy of the psychiatrist. The odds are that you'll remain aware enough to make intelligent choices about your treatment.

Actually, problems for which most people seek professional help are not even close to incapacitating. They're disorders such as impotence, nagging and unreasonable fears, family conflicts, occupational problems, and the like. Such people aren't psychotic, and are even able to continue working and otherwise continue with their lives while trying to overcome their difficulties.

One way to find a psychiatrist or counselor who can help you is a referral from your family doctor, if you trust his judgment. Even so, be careful. When you go for your first visit, look him over as carefully as he scrutinizes you. Don't be too impressed by any diplomas or certificates hanging on his wall. These are often mere window dressing. It's critically important to understand that certificates are merely part of the office decor, arranged to impress patients. Office decor, which includes family photos, the arrangement of chairs, and even a plant, is designed to create a warm, homey effect.[23]

In fact, certificates are about as meaningful as driver's licenses. They only prove that the holder passed a test or met a set of requirements some time ago. They definitely do not prove that he's competent today.

Look, and listen carefully when the shrink outlines a course of treatment for you. If he suggests electric shock treatment or anything that drastic as first choice, run like hell! This is definitely the moment to get a second opinion.

If he prescribes a drug, check it out in a reference source at the library before taking the first pill. Several sources, such as the *Physician's Desk Reference*, and *The Pill Book*, list dosages, effects, and side-effects of prescription drugs.

Don't just take his word for it when you ask him about side-effects. Be very careful if he pooh-poohs your concern about side-effects. He's being dishonest, because ALL DRUGS HAVE SIDE-EFFECTS.

While taking the drug, monitor yourself carefully for side-effects. Be especially careful if you drive or operate machinery of any sort. Some psychoactive drugs have weird effects, and can be as incapacitating as alcohol, but more subtle. Haldol, for example, causes blurred vision in some people, even in small doses. You might feel fine, not "dopey," but your vision will be less acute. This can be dangerous while driving.

A very important fact to remember is that drug side-effects are usually reversible. They tend to vanish when the patient reduces his dose or stops completely. The side-effects of ECT and psychosurgery tend to be permanent, because these "treatments" actually cause brain damage.

If the suggested treatment is "psychotherapy" or "counseling," you're on relatively safe ground, because the main danger is to your wallet. A therapist can harm you only if you allow him to, and we'll lay out some cautions later in this chapter. However, be aware that you can spend quite a bit of money without corresponding benefit, and that it's very hard to pin down the cost-effectiveness of psychotherapy.

Also keep in mind that, with a limited budget, cost-effectiveness is very important. In this regard, those listed as "counselors" can be as helpful as psychiatrists. A counselor is a non-medical graduate of a psychological counseling program, and has a master's or higher degree in psychology. A psychiatrist is a medical doctor who specializes in psychological problems. As a specialist, he gets a higher fee than a family doctor. The main difference between a psychiatrist and a counselor is that the medical doctor can prescribe drugs. If you need help for a problem, a counselor will cost you less.

Malpractice and Fraud

Psychiatry and psychotherapy are not sciences, and it's necessary to remain alert to the prospects of malpractice, exploitation, and even fraud. It's definitely "buyer beware."

If you see a shrink of any sort, always keep the relationship on a professional level. Here are some warning signs that things are not on an even keel:

♦ The shrink who wants to do another kind of business with you, selling you cosmetics, real estate, or other consumer goods. Remember, a counselor is a shrink, not a Fuller Brush Man or Avon Lady!

♦ The shrink who tries to start a sexual relationship with you. Even the biggest names in the field aren't above this. Jules Masserman, noted American psychiatrist, recently lost a lawsuit for precisely this sort of unprofessional behavior. Sexual exploitation has become such a problem that eleven states have now passed laws against sexual abuse by therapists.[24]

♦ The shrink who refuses to provide any sort of estimate regarding how long psychotherapy will take. He may only be willing to spend several hours a week with you until the cash cow runs dry.

♦ The shrink who talks endlessly about his problems. You're paying him to focus on your problems, not use you as a sounding board for his personal hang-ups.

♦ The shrink who bullies you. If you become the victim of a shrink who uses you as an emotional punching bag, you're in the hands of someone whose problems are worse than yours.

◆ The shrink who remains too aloof, out of touch and remote, and therefore unavailable in a crisis. If your shrink won't return phone calls in an emergency, watch out! While a shrink may feel put upon by patients' problems, and be reluctant to advise patients during off-duty hours, this goes with the territory. It's very much like becoming a parent obliges a person to learn how to change diapers, unattractive as this chore may be.

◆ The shrink whose treatment plan drags on, with no end in sight. Conversely, watch out for the shrink who tells you that you've made marvelous progress and are ready for discharge, right after you inform him that you're running out of money.

Finally, if all else fails, go see your bartender. Despite the lack of "professional" credentials, bartenders are good practical psychologists, and many generations have used them for informal "therapy" and gotten away with nothing worse than a hang-over.

Notes:

1. *Time*, November 29, 1993, p. 49.
2. *Uses and Abuses of Psychology*, H. J. Eysenck, Baltimore, MD, Penguin Books, 1953, pp. 195-208.
3. *U. S. News & World Report*, May 24, 1993, p. 58.
4. *Time*, November 29, 1993, p. 47.
5. *Uses and Abuses of Psychology*, p. 195.
6. *Ibid.*, pp. 229-230.
7. *Ibid.*, p. 236.
8. *U. S. News & World Report*, May 24, 1993, p. 58.
9. "The Patient's Right to Effective Treatment: Implications of Osheroff v. Chestnut Lodge," *American Journal of Psychiatry*, April, 1990, v147, p. 409.
10. *Shock Treatment, Psychosurgery, and Other Somatic Treatments in Psychiatry*, Lothar B. Kalinowski, M. D., and Paul D. Hoch, M. D., NY, Grune & Stratton, 1952. This was the major work at the time, and the cataloging of psychiatric classifications treated by both ECT and psychosurgery is visible just by scanning the book's title page.

11. Equally bizarre was the personal history of Antonio Egas Moniz, the neurologist who devised lobotomy during the early 1930s, for which he received a belated Nobel Prize in 1949. His career was colorful, and he once served as Portugal's foreign minister. Ironically, he ended his days violently, shot to death by one of his lobotomized patients.
12. Kalinowski and Hoch, *op.cit.* Psychosurgery, because it wasn't as quick and easy to apply as ECT, had far fewer uses, but nevertheless at least 100,000 people in this country had psychosurgery of one sort or another during its disreputable history.
13. *Uses and Abuses of Psychology*, pp. 195-200.
14. *U. S. News & World Report*, May 24, 1993, p. 61.
15. "Depression: Younger Patients, Newer Therapies," Patricia Thomas, *Medical World News*, August, 1990, v. 31, no. 14, p. 28.
16. "Depression: What Can be Done?," *Health Facts*, January, 1990, v15, p. 1.
17. *Disease-Mongers*, Lynn Payer, NY, 1992, John Wiley & Sons, p. 234.
18. *Nu City*, November 19, 1993, p. 3.
19. *Information Please Almanac*, Boston, Houghton Miflin Company, 1993, p. 545.
20. *Security Management*, January, 1994, p. 48.
21. *Time,* November 29, 1993, p. 52.
22. *Time*, November 29, 1993, p. 56.
23. "Designing Doctors," *The Edell Health Letter*, August, 1990, v9, p. 7.
24. *U.S. News & World Report,* May 24, 1993, p. 61.

Chapter 13
The Trouble With Lawyers

There's a bitter joke that reflects the feelings of many Americans about lawyers:

A lawyer dies and arrives at the Pearly Gates. Saint Peter greets him warmly, and asks him to wait while a ten-room suite is being prepared for him. As he's waiting, the Pope appears, having just died. Referring to his clipboard, Saint Peter tells the Pope to proceed to the dormitory reserved for Popes. The lawyer, surprised, asks Saint Peter why he's putting the Pope in a dormitory while he, a mere lawyer, is allotted a ten-room suite. Saint Peter replies, "Hey, I've got several dozen Popes up here. You're the only lawyer."

On a more serious note, James Kilpatrick's column of October 22, 1985, criticized the role of the lawyers in the Bhopal incident, in which toxic fumes from a Union Carbide plant poisoned the area. About 3,500 people were killed, and about 200,000 others sustained a variety of ailments from exposure to the fumes. Soon after the accident, American lawyers arrived, carrying on the strong "ambulance-chasing" tradition.

This is only one incident, although a very newsworthy one. It demonstrates the problems with the American legal "profession," and why its members behave more like members of organized crime than true professionals.

The basic problems with lawyers are:

1. Like doctors, they form a self-protective brotherhood purportedly concerned with maintaining "professional standards," while its real agenda is devoted to higher earnings.
2. Like psychologists and psychiatrists, they deal in intangibles. Furthermore, because the law is based on notions of "right" and "wrong," the field's wide open for abuses as well as sincere differences of interpretations.
3. Like doctors, psychologists, and psychiatrists, lawyers work by the hour, providing a strong financial incentive to increase their earnings by spinning out a case through the lengthy and convoluted appeals process. Most of our laws contribute to the "full employment for lawyers" agenda. The reason?
4. All of our judges, many of our legislators, all of our prosecutors, and even some of our presidents are lawyers. All have titles, some reeking of the stature of European nobility. We address judges as "Your Honor," a relic of British practice, where British judges enjoy titles such as "Your Lordship."

Why Do We Need Them, Anyway?

For many centuries, the law was within the understanding of the common man. This was necessary, because understanding the law was a prerequisite for obeying it. This simple, common-sense principle showed itself in the uncomplicated structures of our traditional codes of behavior, such as the Hammurabic Code, the Ten Commandments and others. To run an ordered society, the law had to be simple and understandable, even to illiterates, and most people were illiterate in ancient and medieval times. Unfortunately, the law and its practitioners evolved, and today the law is too complicated for any single person to understand. This is why we need the "experts."[1]

Sometimes, the law can be ridiculous. The old New York State Penal code, scrapped in 1969 for a new one, had a category called "Wayward Minor," a curious mixture of Victorian morality and criminal justice. This section stated that a juvenile was a "wayward minor," subject to the authority of juvenile court, if he engaged in any of fourteen forms of behavior. Among these were: disobeying parents, running away from home, frequenting "bad companions," using foul language, masturbation, and truancy from school.

The law is the way it is because it's a crazy-quilt of prejudices, obsolete ideas, amendments, and special favors for influential campaign contributors. Obsolete laws, such as those making adultery and fornication felonies, remain on the books even though they're unenforceable and actually hardly anyone is ever prosecuted for ever violating them. The reason is that legislators, craven cowards that they are, don't want members of fundamentalist church groups voting against them next election.

The Internal Revenue Code, which affects anyone who earns anything, is a legislative horror impossible for any one person to read and understand thoroughly.[2] Despite certain efforts purporting to simplify the paperwork, such as the 1986 tax code, filling out a tax return is a job for a specialist. The new withholding form was so complicated that almost nobody understood it, and it had to be revised and simplified. The "short forms" provided by the IRS are really "Catch-22s," because anyone using them loses hundreds or thousands of dollars in deductions.

That the law is so complicated and hard to understand is no accident. Lawyers keep it that way, to ensure their job security. What other reason could there be for the fine print, so hard to read and understand? What other need is there for boilerplate legal language and phrases such as "party of the first part," "party of the second part," etc.? Lawyers, like doctors, have their protective jargon, designed to keep the common folk from understanding the law.[3]

Legal Tactics

A good criminal lawyer, motivated by enough money, can "beat" almost any rap. Familiar with all of the legal tricks of delay and obfuscation, he can at least get his client's sentence reduced or suspended, even after a conviction. Tactics are similar in both civil and criminal cases.

The first tactic is to delay the proceedings as long as possible. A good lawyer digs up every pretext the law allows to delay the trial, claiming he's unfamiliar with the case, or needs time to locate witnesses. In the last resort, he'll advise his client to secure a further delay by changing lawyers, tossing the case to a colleague who in turn requests a further delay to familiarize himself with the case.

There are several reasons to delay a trial. First is that witnesses forget, move away, and even die. A police officer may quit or retire. The prosecutor may be promoted, or leave for private practice, and the new prosecutor has to learn the case. Time works for the defendant.

We see this typically in cases involving insurance companies. The typical insurance company has a staff of lawyers following a program of routinely delaying cases as long as possible, because experience shows that this policy pays off on the average. Plaintiffs die, move away, or become so sick and tired of the whole thing that they drop their cases or accept settlement offers. Interminable delay is also a coercive tactic for insurance companies, because they present the plaintiff with a dilemma — accept their terms, or wait years to collect.

Keep in mind that, even if you're affluent enough to afford a lawyer, you may get the same cheap and dirty justice. In criminal cases, your lawyer gets his money up front. With your money in his pocket, he has no financial incentive to put out more than a token effort, and may advise you to go for a plea-bargain. On the other hand, he may make a maximum effort because of his own integrity, but integrity is rare among lawyers.

The situation is even more cruel if your lawyer, knowing from experience that you haven't got a chance, advises going for a trial because this will provide him a bigger fee. He'll stick you for the money up front, of course, knowing that you're going to be convicted. No guarantees, remember.

The Cost of Lawyers

Why is our criminal justice system so inefficient? Why did the man who shot the Pope get tried, convicted, and sentenced in an Italian court while Hinckley, accused of shooting President Reagan, was still awaiting trial? Why was Claus von Bulow, convicted of murder, able to hire Alan Dershowitz, Dean of the Harvard Law School, to get him a new trial in which he was acquitted?

The reason is that the law in this country has become perverted. It no longer exists to maintain order and keep society on the rails. Today, it exists solely for the convenience and profit of the lawyers. Inefficiency is allowable, and even desirable, because it's immensely profitable.

The old saying is that, "There's one law for the rich, and another for the poor." While not perfectly accurate, this dictum reflects the fact that the quality of legal representation you get in court is usually directly related to how much you can spend. You still have your "constitutional rights," but it'll cost you a bundle to exercise them. The whole point and purpose of our legal system today is to earn generous incomes for lawyers, not to serve either their clients or society as a whole.

Notes:

1. *The Screwing of the Average Man*, David Hapgood, NY, Doubleday & Company, 1974, p. 81.
2. *Guerrilla Capitalism*, Adam Cash, Port Townsend, WA, Loompanics Unlimited, 1984.
3. *The Screwing of the Average Man*, p. 81.

Part Three:
Defense And Counter-Attack

Throughout the preceding chapters, we've studied the ways of individual and institutionalized fraud, and outlined methods of self-protection. However, sometimes averting the fraud isn't enough. What about the person who has been victimized by a con man so clever that he slips away from the law? Retaliation is important, as well, to preserve psychological equilibrium.

We're also going to study pro-active defense, which in plain language means "hit them first." At times, a pre-emptive attack is the best way to go. Let's get into the nitty-gritty.

Chapter 14
Striking Back At Con Artists

If a con artist tries to victimize you, avoiding being scammed may seem to be sufficient. However, this merely protects your financial interest, but leaves the confidence artist free to victimize someone else. Taking positive, pro-active steps against the con artist cramps his style, wastes his time, and can serve as a deterrent next time he contemplates executing one of his cons.

Attitude

What you choose to do depends largely upon your attitudes toward crime, criminals, the effectiveness of our police, and the place of the citizen in seeking justice in this country. A very popular view is to do nothing, to allow the criminal to get away with it, and to count your blessings that he didn't take you for more than he did. The "logic" behind this is that your life is worth more than the contents of your wallet, but as there's rarely any physical danger to the victim in con games, this train of thought doesn't apply here.

The person who only avoids being scammed doesn't really solve the problem, except in a very narrow, self-interested way. He's merely sent the problem on to somebody else. The person who cripples the scam artist's operation, on the other hand, performs a positive task for the good of his country, and can congratulate himself on a job well done.

More important than your duty to society is your psychological equilibrium. This depends upon your self-image, the way you prefer to see yourself. Do you want to see yourself as a potential or actual victim, running scared, feeling helpless against criminal aggression? Do you feel that nothing can be done, because the police are ineffective against most crime, anyway? If this is your mind-set, don't be surprised if you begin to suffer depression, and feelings of unworthiness, after any criminal victimization, especially if the police fail to apprehend the criminal. You'll end up demoralized, your faith in truth and justice destroyed, because you'll have left yourself, in fact, defenseless against victimization.

If, on the other hand, you resent someone walking over you, and are prepared not only to resist but to strike back, you're in a much better position psychologically. This attitude demonstrates a certain self-confidence, and self-reliance, that makes you less dependent upon the police, courts, and other agencies of social order.

The Case For Action

Some might hesitate to take positive action against confidence artists, feeling that all law enforcement should be left up to the police, and that a citizen becomes a vigilante if he does any more than report a crime to police. This is a narrow-minded and unrealistic view, for several reasons.

First, let's consider the role of the police. Except for the rare crime, the police almost never catch a criminal in the act. Their role is limited to taking reports, and trying to "solve" what crimes they can. Today, police are so overwhelmed that the most serious crime of all, murder, has a solution rate of only about 67 percent. Property crimes have much lower solution rates, with burglary and larceny down around 13 percent. Frauds are so unimportant that they're not even listed in the FBI's annual reports, and thus no national figures are available. The bottom line is that, if you're the victim of fraud, you'll be very lucky if the police can do anything except generate more paperwork.

Second, today's fraud artist is alert and aware that avoiding criminal prosecution depends on being an elusive target. Fast-moving is his lifestyle, and often the intended victim is the only person who can take effective action against him. Even so, the window of opportunity is open only temporarily, and if you're to act effectively, you have to decide and move quickly. Getting official agencies to act is often time-consuming, especially as they have more important crimes, such as murder and mugging, on their plates.

Finally, there's the practical point that, if you don't do it, it won't get done. Many people adopt a "not my job" attitude, which appears expedient and convenient in the short run, but is self-destructive in the long run. "What goes around, comes around," and the criminal you let go today may be back tomorrow to victimize your relatives, neighbors, and friends. Also to the point is that the criminal another potential victim fails to stop will be making you his next target.

Strategy

To act effectively against the next con artist you encounter, you need to have an overall plan, a sense of direction, as a basis for the specific actions you'll take. If you have a "killer instinct," you'll take to the more aggressive methods, going beyond mere self-protection into no-holds-barred, aggressive counter-attack.

If this is your outlook, you must be prepared for a vigorous, aggressive effort. You won't just be listening while your telephone answering machine screens your calls, or merely asking for identification when an "inspector" comes to examine your furnace. Instead, you'll be seeking to sucker him in and lead him on, to give you an opportunity to savage him with his own methods.

On the surface, the attitude you display will be one of friendly alertness when meeting any stranger. Most strangers are indeed, harmless, but you have to be prepared for the occasional con artist. You must remain alert and aware without seeming suspicious. A ready smile goes a long way toward lulling a con artist's self-protective impulses.

The purpose of many techniques will be to waste the con artist's time. Time is precious to legitimate and dishonest salesmen alike, and the more of their time you can waste, the more you'll crimp their plans. This is why you'll no longer simply hang up when a salesman calls during supper. If you cut him short, he'll merely move on to another prospect. Your purpose is to waste more of his time than he's wasting of yours.

Some techniques will allow you to cause severe complications for the fraud artist, worse than hanging on the phone for a couple of minutes, or the annoyance of a missed appointment. You'll be able to incite criminal prosecution in some cases, and bring violence to his door in others. We'll cover these techniques in detail.

Preparation

You'll need certain practical tools for messing up a swindler. The basic tools are a pad and pen, which you'll keep with you at all times. You'll need to record:

1. Numbers of public telephones, some of which will be in remote places such as road-side booths.
2. Addresses of abandoned buildings.
3. Names, addresses, and telephone numbers of people you dislike.
4. The telephone number of the local police bunco squad, and the public prosecutor in charge of fraud. Usually, these have separate numbers, not going through the agency switchboard.

Some paperwork will help in certain situations. Having business cards under a false identity is one way to do it, but most of us have opportunities to pick up other people's business cards in the normal course of events. Such cards will do fine.

Keep an eye out for a lost credit card or checkbook. You may find one on the street, in a park, or other public place. You may find one next to a garbage can or dumpster. Pick it up and save it. It can be invaluable in making fake "deposits" in a swindle.

Know your local geography. At least, learn the location and lay-out of a hotel with several exits, because this will allow you to "ditch" a con artist.

Tell Lies

An additional tool, one that you may have to develop, is the ability to lie easily and naturally. You have to be able to lie convincingly about matters that may seem trivial to you, and about which people don't usually lie. Let's see why, by looking at a few examples:

A panhandler approaches you in a hallway in the building where you work. You tell him that you left your wallet at home, but that you'll swing by home to get it, on the way to your next "call." You do not tell the panhandler that you work at that address, but that you are a "consultant" or "repairman" (depending on what you're wearing) who makes several calls a day. Tell him that you'll meet him in two hours at a building several blocks away. He may or may not fall for your story, but your adept lie has put him on the horns of a dilemma.

It will be more convincing if you mention the name of a specific company where you'll be "visiting" in two hours' time. Adding a telephone number may be worthwhile. He just may waste a quarter asking for you.

Another common situation is the telephone sales artist who "pitches" you and asks for your name and address for delivery. Give him the address of a mail drop (keep a couple of these in your notebook), because that will delay things for him. If you were to give him the name and address of a real person, that individual would refuse the shipment immediately. Likewise if you were to provide a non-existent address. A mail drop receives so many envelopes and packages each day that the operator doesn't scrutinize them individually until he puts them in each box. He may hand the package back to the carrier the next day, or it may lie in a corner for a week if the mail drop is particularly busy.

To lie effectively and without hesitation, you must have a prepared set of lies and cover stories that can roll off your tongue easily. You need to be able to cover several basic situations, such as explaining why you can't come up with the required amount of money immediately, or why you can't accompany the con artist at that moment.

Some easy lies that cover many situations are:

1. You left your wallet at home, or in your desk or locker at work.
2. You don't have that much cash with you.
3. You have only one checkbook or credit card, and your spouse has it today. You can both use it, because you have the same first initials, and the card simply says "J. Frank." That's not your real name but so what?
4. You left your traveler's checks in the hotel safe.

The Basic Tactics

Whenever a fraud artist accosts you, the first tactic is never to act on his proposal at the outset. Always find an excuse to postpone action, even though you seem to be in complete agreement with him. The above-cited example of how to deal with the panhandler is one way to do it. If nothing else, excuse yourself to go to the bathroom. Be sure you have an array of basic and realistic roadblocks to avoid immediate action. This gives you time to think, and to set up a complication for him.

Never, never, never say that you're "busy." This is such an obviously stale and phony excuse that it won't fool anyone for a moment. Instead, use other excuses that sound compelling, and that indicate willingness to cooperate with the fraud artist.

For example, use one of the following to indicate compliance, but to produce a delay:

1. "I'd like to, but I'm on my way to a doctor's appointment. Can we get together afterwards?"
2. "I'm picking up my child at school. I'll be free in an hour."
3. "I'm going to visit my wife (mother, aunt, child, etc.) in the hospital. I'll be home by ____o'clock."

Such delaying tactics work well against an "inspector" or other fraud artist who appears at your door. Use an excuse, and tell him to return in an hour.

The tactic of delay and counter-proposal is far better than to simply say, "I'm not interested." If a con man hits you with a pigeon-drop scheme, and asks you to go your bank to withdraw "earnest money," agree, but delay. Tell him you'll meet him at your bank after your doctor's appointment. If he buys your story, you'll have sent him on a fool's errand. Naturally, don't send him to your bank, but to another far across town.

It helps to have a false identity ready to support your tactics. The fake I.D. can be very thin, because it will never need to pass official scrutiny. A few business cards are often enough.

Having the number of a public phone handy is very helpful here. Keep one of these memorized, ready for any con man who asks for your number. The reason it should be the number of a pay phone in a remote area is that the chance of anyone answering is smaller than if it were in a shopping mall. The con man should have to ring it many times, waiting for you to arrive "home" to answer.

One benefit of a delaying tactic is that it gives you time to call police. If you're fairly sure that the person is a swindler and his scheme's open to prosecution, don't hesitate to call police. If you're able to tell the bunco officer that you've arranged for the con artist to return at a specific time, you can be sure to get his attention. He or another officer will be there to cover you and witness the attempted swindle.

When the Phone Rings

Pick up the phone eagerly. Even if the sales call comes during supper, it's an opportunity to strike at either a telemarketer, who is a rude pest, or a telescammer. Listen willingly to the pitch. If the caller addresses you by name, it's a clue that he got your name and number from the telephone directory, not by random dialing. Tell him that although you've still got the same phone number, you've moved. Give him an address across town when he sets up an appointment either to ship the product or to give you a home demonstration. The address, of course, may be that of an abandoned building, or a police station. A mental hospital would be even funnier.

Another way to waste his time is to tell him that the person he's trying to reach is no longer at the number or address, but that you'd like to hear the details. Of course, you give a false name and address. This is where your prepared false identity comes in handy as you read from your notebook.

People try to sell the most amazing products by phone, even big-ticket items that were sold only in retail stores a few years ago. A good way to cross up any of these phone solicitors is to agree to buy whatever they're selling. Keep in mind that you don't sign anything over the phone, and can later deny that you bought anything. Here's where the little credit card white lie helps, if the salesman asks you for your credit card number.

If payment by credit card is impossible, the salesman may ask you to pay by check. Tell him that you'll mail it to him, and ask for the address of the company. Let's call it "Advanced Associates." Write it down, and save it for later. Of course, you don't send a check, unless you happen to have an old checkbook found in the street.

If you have some time free, and decide to play with him on the phone for awhile, you can give him a made-up credit card number. He'll check it out on his computer terminal with the bank, and find that it doesn't register. When he tells you this, stick to your guns. Ask him if he's got the number right, and have him read it back to you. When he does, inform him that he'd copied one digit wrong, and run him through the whole procedure again. If he tells you again that it doesn't compute, tell him that the computer must be in error, and ask if he can send it C.O.D.

Delivery can be the fun part, because you have several choices. One is to send him to the wrong address. Another is to tell him that delivery will have to be on a weekend. Saying that both you and your wife work during the week is a convincing story. This can cause him trouble in scheduling, especially if the item's a water softener or other appliance requiring installation. Propose that delivery and installation be in the evening. If he can't agree to that, rebut by suggesting that delivery be on a weekend.

If he sticks to his guns, insisting that delivery must be during business hours, he'll probably ask that you leave your key and payment with a neighbor. This provides the opportunity to string him along some more. You have two choices here:

1. You can tell him that you've just moved in, and don't know any of your neighbors.
2. You can agree, saying that you have to ask your neighbors to find out which one will be home at the day and time he proposes to deliver. Tell him you'll call him back after arranging the time with a neighbor, and ask him for a telephone number where you can reach him. The odds are that he won't give you one, instead stating that he'll call you back in an hour. If you have an answering machine, screen your calls and simply let him eat his heart out trying to reach you.

Yet another way to savage a salesman is to agree to delivery the day and time he proposes. Tell him that you or your wife will be home that day. Of course, when the truck arrives, nobody is home to accept delivery. When the salesman calls to find out why, you have your story ready: "Gee, I'm sorry, but my wife's aunt got hit by a car that morning, and she had to go to the hospital. Can you bring it by next week?"

When you get tired of the comedy, you can end the routine by telling him that you weren't home because you forgot the item was coming. Other endings are:

1. "A water softener? I've already got one, and don't need another."
2. "My wife? I don't know what you're talking about. I'm not married."
3. "I don't have a credit card. It was canceled last year when I declared bankruptcy. You must have me confused with somebody else."
4. "No, it couldn't have been me. I just moved in yesterday."

What about the address of his company, which you wrote down when you said you'd send him a check? Go to a stationery store and have a rubber stamp made, with the salesman's name (it's probably fictitious, anyway) and the company's address. Round up all of the magazine subscription cards you can find, stamp them with the new stamp, and drop them in the mail. This will flood their mailbox with magazines, a standard harassment tactic that still works today.

The Fake Charity

This situation is perfect for the fake check. If you receive a solicitation from a suspicious-seeming "charity" in the mail, by all means return it with a check, but on a closed account, or from a checkbook you found in the street. This is especially good if the "charity" supplies a post-paid business reply envelope.

Ditching or Stranding

Another nasty technique is stranding the con man. Get him to accompany you in your car on a pretext, such as visiting your aunt in the hospital. When you get there, tell him that your aunt's in intensive care, and only family are allowed. Ask him to wait for you in the lobby, and leave the hospital by another exit.

You should be aware that using this technique can bring two problems. One is that you might not even want him in your car at any time. The other is that he may wait for you at your car, or watch your vehicle from the lobby.

If the con man accosts you in the street, whatever his line may be, one counter-measure is to tell him that you're traveling, and ask him to walk with you to your hotel. Don't let him come up to your room, on the pretext that your "wife" is sleeping. As we've noted, a hotel is perfect for ditching because it typically has several entrances. While he's awaiting you in the lobby, leave by a side door.

Planting Contraband

If you have a source of illegal drugs, you have a beautiful opportunity to "frame" a swindler. Don't try this unless you're already into recreational illegal drugs yourself, and have a reliable source. Otherwise, you invite the risk of running into a police snitch or undercover officer while trying to make a buy.

A cruel variation on the theme of calling police is workable if an arrest actually comes down. It helps to plan ahead, and if you have a large manila envelope, with a glassine envelope of cocaine inside, you can drive another nail into the fraud artist's coffin. Just before the police take him away, you go into another room, bring out the envelope, and say, "I just remembered. He forgot this when he was here before." Of course, you don't want your fingerprints anywhere inside the envelope.

It would help greatly if his prints were inside, though. You can arrange this in some instances. If the bunco artist tries to hand you some sales literature on the first encounter, accept it, but don't touch it. Simply tell him to put it on the table, and that you'll look at it later. Pack this inside the large envelope, using gloves, while waiting for the police.

Another ploy is to ask him for an envelope or a sheet of paper on a pretext. Again, you ask him to put it down, and thank him. Again, it goes inside the large envelope after he leaves.

The opportunities for planting evidence are endless. Let's look at them further.

In many of the contacts you'll have with swindlers, you'll have opportunities to "plant" contraband on one or more of them. If the swindler comes to your home to sell you some phony "investments," you can take his coat to hang in the closet, playing the good host. If you're married, it's easy to do this while your spouse holds the swindler's attention.

If he doesn't have an outer coat, he may have a briefcase. Distracting him while your spouse plants a small envelope of contraband in his briefcase serves the purpose.

In some instances, such as land fraud, the swindler will want to drive you to the site. This is usually a large tract of land with only a couple of buildings on it, but the con artist promises that one day soon, a large development will occupy the site. You may slip an envelope under the seat of the car. When you get out, note carefully if he locks his car.

Once the evidence is planted, call the police from a public phone, to avoid having the call traced to your line.[1] Ask for the narco officer. Your pitch goes like this:

"I got some information for you. John Smith's walking around with an ounce of (heroin, hash, cocaine, etc.) and he keeps it in his _____. You can find him at _____."

Narcotics officers are accustomed to receiving anonymous tips. Often, they originate with a drug dealer's competitor who uses the police to eliminate his rival. Although the officer may ask your name, you can give an alias or just state that you're someone who's no friend of "Smith's." The officer won't ignore your tip. If he tries to bluff you by claiming he can't do anything unless he knows your name, tell him right out:

"Hey, I've got my own reasons for not giving you my name. Take it or leave it."

The ideal situation is if the officer can verify the information without needing a search warrant. Although the law requires a search warrant in most instances, police often finesse their way past this by a stratagem. To do this, they must be able to search illegally without getting caught. If the preliminary search discloses evidence, they can obtain a search warrant to cover a more extensive search. They simply make up "probable cause" to satisfy the judge who signs the warrant.

If the "evidence" is on the person, or in a briefcase, it's not as convenient as if it were in a motor vehicle. If your swindler neglects to lock his car, tell this to the police, as it will make it much easier for them. If he locks his car, plant the "evidence" under his bumper or in a fender well, using a magnetic key holder. As long as a narco officer can find the evidence without too much trouble and without a search warrant, your chances of "framing" the swindler on a narcotics charge are very good.[2]

Finale

The foregoing scenarios lay out a few ways in which you might strike back at con artists, hitting hard enough to draw blood. If you ask, "Why draw blood?" then you possibly don't realize that criminals don't care if they spill *your* blood, because criminals are sociopaths. Basically, criminals don't have consciences, and this justifies remorseless counter-measures.

The difficulty of prosecuting swindlers is so great that the machinery of law and order, creaky as it is, needs a little help from concerned citizens. Simple self-defense and avoidance of scams can protect you, but such passive precautions merely pass the problem on to others. Some of these will surely be less well-equipped than you to defend themselves. Active measures, such as described in this section, ensure that the swindler doesn't get away scot-free, and in some instances can be prosecuted for a more serious charge. Whatever it takes, anything which cripples a swindler's operation, or gets him put away for a few years, benefits society.

Notes:

1. Many people still don't know this, but all police "911" consoles display the caller's number on the screen. Many other numbers in a police station are linked to this, and police can quickly find out from which number a call to them originates.
2. Police and courts take narcotics offenses much more seriously than they do bunco charges.

Chapter 15
How To Make Rip-Offs
Work For You

Throughout most of this book, our topic of study has been rip-offs people may inflict on you, and how to avoid becoming a victim. The emphasis has been on rip-offs as criminal activities, used by ruthless people to prey on others.

Now let's look at the other side of the coin. Rip-off techniques can work in your favor, even if you're not a law-breaker. Deception and cheating are widespread, and we can even consider them normal in many aspects of our lives.[1]

In one sense, deception is the weapon of the weak against the strong who bully them. It's a form of guerrilla warfare that the underdog uses in self-defense.

The Ethics of Deception

We all have a sense of morality, even the career criminals among us. A con artist, for example, would not rob a bank at gun-point, although he'd eagerly extract the bank's money by a scam. A murderer might not stoop to molesting a child. Like the criminal elements, the rest of us have our own moralities, which don't necessarily accord with the written law. In some ways, we consider deception as part of our lives, and we think it essential to preserve lifestyle and dignity. This is the defensive aspect of deception.

Some people, for example, consider income tax to be an unfair imposition by a government that's gotten too big and too powerful, and so they openly advocate methods of avoiding taxes.[2] Tax cheating is illegal, and some consider it immoral. Yet, there's one important distinction to make between tax cheating and passing a false check and other scams. The criminal attempts to take what belongs to another. The defensive cheater tries to keep what's his against a greater power's effort to compel him to surrender it.

We can draw a parallel with stealing from an employer. While it's vital to understand that some thieving employees steal simply out of greed and acquisitiveness, many others steal to "get what's theirs." Some people work for abusive employers, who treat employees unfairly and even brutally, under cover of their role as boss. Some employers are "acting out" personalities, who inflict their miseries and neuroses on their subordinates. Others are simply vicious exploiters who try to squeeze as much as they can from their employees, while giving as little as possible in return. With employers such as these, it's not surprising that some employees quickly become "burned out."

Some employees may well feel that their boss deserves what's coming to him. One who pays sub-standard wages, withholds promised raises and benefits, is likewise double-dealing his employees, and cheating him is either a defensive move or a counter-attack. It's a way to promote a deserved but unawarded bonus, or a way to get revenge.

Similarly, the employer who demands "loyalty" from his employees, while unwilling to give them his loyalty, provokes a feeling of being unjustly treated among his employees. A conspicuous and widespread example is the employer who demands two weeks' notice from employees who quit, but who gives two minutes' notice when laying off.

Institutionalized Corruption

In some countries, such as Mexico and Nigeria, public employees are so poorly paid that gratuities are a large part of their incomes. This is semi-legitimate. Although accepting a tip or bribe may be against the rules, everyone does it and that makes corruption institutionalized. To an American, it may seem strange to have to tip a clerk at City Hall for a building permit or a bicycle license, but that's the "system" in some countries. In this country, some poorly-paid employees also seek to augment their take-homes by irregular means.

Revenge

Revenge is another aspect of rule-breaking. There have been notable instances of vengeful employees and ex-employees sabotaging their employers. Some have destroyed machinery and supplies, while others have destroyed records in file cabinets. The most elegant method of inflicting destruction is the "logic bomb," placed into the company computer.

The logic bomb works only if the employee can re-program or insert a set of hidden instructions into his employer's computer. The instructions monitor the payroll account, and if the employee's name is expunged from the payroll, the computer's memory is erased.[3] Thus, the ex-employee gets back at the boss who canned him, whatever the reason.

Defensive Cheating

We see that cheating is justified when the rules are unfair by being stacked against the employee. This is very commonplace, and because it's woven into our lifestyle, we often do it without being completely aware of it. Let's examine a few examples to see how almost everybody cheats defensively:

- An employee slips a company pen and pad of paper into his pocket. If you ask him why, he may say: "That cheapskate boss has a lot of them. My kid needs this to do her homework."
- An underpaid photographer moonlights on the side, and uses company facilities and supplies to make the photographs he sells to his customers. He's been doing this for years, and most of the photographers he knows also do it.
- A man goes to his doctor, complaining of weakness and spots before his eyes. The doctor puts him in the hospital for extensive tests, which disclose a severe disease for which there is no treatment, but which usually goes into remission after a few weeks. The doctor tells his patient: "I'm going to put down that you have an ulcer, and prescribe some pills for it. That way, you'll be covered by Blue Cross. They don't pay hospital bills just for tests and diagnosis, only for treatment."[4]
- An out-of-work employee collects unemployment insurance benefits while trying to find another job. The payments are too small to support his family, and to make ends meet, so he works several nights a week for a friend, taking payment in cash and not reporting it to the government. Is he wrong?
- A mechanic, who sees his paycheck growing more slowly than taxes and inflation, and who has to support a wife and two children, gets the uneasy feeling that the system is screwing him. Working at a second job during his evenings, he doesn't report this income on his tax return, and now has regained the effective spending power he had five years ago. Although the IRS complains that it lost $35 billion this way in 1976, and $50 billion in 1979,[5] this trend has continued.

"Beating the System"

This is the basis of all defensive deceit, and is what you have to make work for you. To beat the system, you first have to understand it. It's stupid to make a clumsy effort and get caught at the start because you didn't do your homework.

Let's consider an unfavorable situation you may face as an employee. Your immediate supervisor isn't too bad, but company policies are working against you and other employees. You have two choices — open rebellion or stealth.

Open rebellion can take several forms. You can quit in anger, but this brings the problem of finding another job. You can also be stigmatized as a "troublemaker." Always keep in mind: "It's all right to leave, but don't slam the door."

You can join with other employees to organize a union, but this brings you out in the open, and your neck will be sticking out a mile. You can be certain that if your efforts at unionization fail, you're marked. The National Labor Relations Act forbids an employer from firing you for union activity, but it doesn't require him to promote you or award you a pay increase. The net result is that, if you fail, you'll be out in the cold, with your career with that company at a dead end. Finally, you may be surprised to find that the union you bring in is even more exploitative than your company, and that it negotiates a "sweetheart" contract with your boss and forgets about you. These are some reasons why union membership in this country has been steadily dropping since it hit high tide of 40 percent of the American labor force in 1940. Today, fewer than 15 percent of American employees are unionized.

Stealth has its advantages. You know that your boss is waging economic war against you. You're planning to wage war against him, but it'll be an undeclared war, deep in the shadows. His defenses won't be aroused because he won't be aware that you're fighting him.

The first step is to learn about the company. Its formal organization is only the surface structure. What you need to know is its substructure, and you won't learn this by reading the company's employee policy handbook. Study your company's security measures, if any. Learn the weak points, and devise ways to take advantage of them. There are so many possibilities that it's impossible to cover them all. We can, however, study a few successful examples which show how the basic principles work.

♦ A shipping clerk needed his job badly, although aware that his employer was taking advantage of a tight job market during a recession to underpay him. He studied the situation carefully, and found that the stock room, next to the shipping area, had no inventory control, probably because the penny-pinching boss was too cheap to set up a system. While "picking" items from the shelves to fill orders, he was able to appropriate some items for himself, and he smuggled these out during lunch breaks. His wife, who worked elsewhere, sold these items, scissors, needles, and other sewing supplies, to fellow employees.

◆ In the same company, another minimum-wage employee pocketed a shop apron from the sewing room. A sympathetic fellow employee warned him that during manufacture, supplies were counted, and that shortages would show up. His mistake was in acting too soon, before knowing the workings of the company.

◆ A door-to-door salesman was forbidden by his contract to sell competing products, such as Amway, Avon, or Stanley. He carried competitors' catalogs anyway, knowing well that his company had no qualms against using other salesmen to compete against him, even in his own contractual territory. He was successful, earned extra money, and was never caught.

◆ An employee volunteered for the night shift. He knew that, although his employer imposed production quotas, there was no effective supervision during the night shift. This allowed him to produce his quota during the first four hours, then inflate an air mattress and sleep during the rest of his shift.

◆ An office employee had to use the company phone for many long-distance calls during the course of his work. He took advantage of this by making personal long-distance calls at company expense, knowing that there were simply too many long-distance calls to monitor effectively.

◆ Another employee, who'd found management unwilling to reimburse him for damage to his car while on company business, knew that his supervisor counter-signed mileage slips without even looking at them. Over several weeks, he reimbursed himself for the damage by turning in slips for fictitious trips, and inflating the mileage on business trips he did drive.

◆ Yet another employee was forced to cheat to do his job effectively. His employer was so slow in ordering supplies that the employee built up a private stockpile by turning in falsified requisitions. He never sold this material, but used it as a buffer against running out of supplies.

◆ On a night shift in one low-paying company, employees who finished their work left early. A reciprocal agreement among them had the last employee out punching all of the time cards when he left.

◆ One employee volunteered for the night shift because his employer had a liberal policy. If he finished his work early, he could leave and still be paid for eight hours. If his work took him past normal quitting time, he received overtime at the rate of time-and-a-half.

◆ One purchasing agent, severely underpaid for his talent, compared to others in similar positions in nearby companies, had a way of getting back. He awarded contracts to vendors who gave him "kickbacks," and these supplemented his paltry salary.

From these examples, we can derive a few basic principles for success:

1. Understand your employer and his procedures thoroughly.
2. Probe for the weak points. There are always some areas where the employer doesn't exercise complete control, and these permit irregularities in procedure without his ever becoming aware of them. Learn where and when you can "get away" with something.
3. Be discreet, and don't rock the boat. If you're unhappy with the way your employer treats you, don't attract attention by mouthing off. Keep a low profile to avoid attracting attention. Make sure you appear to do your job properly, while also serving your own ends. Meet your production quotas, and act outwardly like a loyal employee. Most importantly, do not brag about getting away with anything. One of those whom you think might be your friends in the company might score points with the boss by stabbing you in the back.
4. Take advantage of a "good slot" if one comes your way. Make luck work for you this way.

None of these methods are extreme. None will make you rich. All will help you nibble away at your problem, and provide an extra margin to help you get along. Use your head, and take advantage when you can.

Notes:

1. *Cheating,* J. Barton Bowyer, NY, St. Martin's Press, 1980, pp. ix, 6.
2. *Guerrilla Capitalism,* Adam Cash, Port Townsend, WA, Loompanics Unlimited, 1984, pp. 5-7.
3. *The Law Enforcement Handbook*, Desmond Rowland and James Bailey, NY, Facts on File Publications, 1985, pp. 260-261.
4. Author's personal experience. This shows that doctors sometimes bend or break the rules out of compassion and concern for their patients.
5. *Cheating*, p. 342.

Chapter 16
Resources

There are many public and private organizations concerned with consumer fraud. On the local level, the police department's fraud squad is one possibility. Many who live in small cities and towns will find that their police department is too small to maintain a detail of specialists, and they have to seek a larger agency to find officers with adequate knowledge of consumer scams. Many state attorneys general operate a consumer fraud division, with state-wide jurisdiction and liaison with other states' enforcement agencies. Finally, private groups provide information regarding whether a particular business or charity is legitimate.

Always remember that prevention is far better than cure. As we've seen, law enforcement agencies assign low priorities to fraud cases, which means that most fraud perpetrators get away with it most of the time. Another consequence is that your chances of recovering what you've lost are small to non-existent. Therefore, if you have any doubt regarding any offer you encounter, check out the person, company, or charity making the solicitation before handing over any of your hard-earned money.

Consumer Information Center
Pueblo, CO 81009

Request Item #640HZ, "Too Good To Be True," a consumer guide to fraud.

Council of Better Business Bureaus
4200 Wilson Blvd., Suite 800
Arlington, VA 22203-1804
Phone: (703) 276-0100

Federal Trade Commission
Sixth St. and Pennsylvania Ave., N. W.
Room 200
Washington, DC 20580
Phone: (202) 326-3277

The FTC regulates a variety of businesses, and can act on complaints regarding certain unethical business practices.

National Charities Information Bureau
19 Union Square West
6th Floor
New York City, NY 10003-3395
Attn: Kenneth L. Albrecht, President
Phone: (212) 929-6300

The NCIB sets standards for charitable fund-raising organizations and accepts complaints and inquiries regarding charitable organizations. This bureau can provide information regarding whether or not a particular charity is legitimate or a fly-by-night.

National Fraud Information Center
(800) 876-7060

This is a source of general information about fraud, and particularly on how to avoid being victimized.

National Insurance Consumer Helpline
(800) 942-4242

This is an industry-sponsored service which can provide answers to common questions about insurance. Don't expect to obtain any dirt, though, as this service is paid for by the industry it covers.

National Insurance Consumer Organization
121 North Payne St.
Alexandria, VA 22314
Phone: (703) 549-8050

This offers a "Buyers Guide to Insurance" and provides advice on pitfalls in buying insurance.

Philanthropic Advisory Service
Council of Better Business Bureaus
4200 Wilson Blvd., Suite 800
Arlington, VA 22203
Attn: James H. McIlhenny, President
Phone: (703) 276-0100

This agency collects information regarding charitable organizations. Contact them for advice regarding a particular philanthropy or charitable organization.

The U.S. Postal Service employs a staff of postal inspectors to combat mail-related frauds. If you think you're the victim of mail fraud, look in the phone book for the number of your local Postal Inspection Service office. You can also ask your postal carrier, or contact:

U.S. Postal Inspection Service
Congressional & Public Affairs Branch
475 L'Enfant Plaza SW
Washington, DC 20260-2160
Phone: (202) 268-4267

The Postal Inspectors have a Postal Crimes Hot Line for those who think they may have been victimized: (800) 654-8896

FAX: (202) 268-4563

The Postal Inspectors are the ones to call if you're the victim of mail fraud. They're more likely to help you than any state or local agency. The Service also publishes a booklet on mail fraud, including health scams.

U.S. Food and Drug Administration
HFE-88 5600 Fishers Lane
Rockville, MD 20857

Weiss Research, Inc.
2200 N. Florida Mango Road
West Palm Beach, FL 33409
Phone: (407) 684-8100

Weiss rates insurance companies, including Blue Cross and Blue Shield, but for the benefit of the customer, not the company or investor.

The *U.S. Pharmacopoeia* is the traditional volume for drug information, but a variety of consumer-oriented publications, written in non-technical language, is available. The section of the Dewey Decimal numbering system, 610 to 620, is about medical topics, and contains a variety of books relating the best and worst doctors, pills, hospitals, etc.

Chapter 17
For Further Reading

Dear America, Melvin Konner, M.D., NY, Addison-Wesley Publishers, 1993. This book is short and sweet, and although its main theme is socialized medicine, Dr. Konner boldly states that there are serious problems in American health care as practiced by the medical establishment today. He documents the problem of unnecessary surgery, citing example after example, making a good case for being wary of surgery. Significantly, he shows one blind spot by neglecting to mention circumcision, the most commonly performed operation in the United States today.

Disease-Mongers, Lynn Payer, NY, 1992, John Wiley & Sons. This is an alarming documentation of organized medical scams, in which doctors and drug companies collaborate and conspire to foist unneeded drugs and unnecessary treatments on patients. Excessive diagnostic testing, hazardous cholesterol-lowering drugs, and other examples of medical hype are ways of extracting more dollars from Americans.

Great Hoaxes, Swindles, Scandals, Cons, Stings, and Scams, Joyce Madison, NY, Penguin Books, 1992. This is an entertaining collection of scammers and imposters, including Ferdinand de Mara, who was so adept at impersonation that he became the subject of a Hollywood movie. More seriously, the author has laid out a variety of scams that affect many people in everyday life. A frightening chapter begins on page 199, a survey of "Doctored Data," examples of medical and other researchers who falsified their studies to attain fame, regardless of any harmful effect on patients.

Sting Shift: The Street-Smart Cop's Handbook of Cons and Swindles, Lindsay E. Smith & Bruce A. Walstad, Littleton, CO, Street-Smart Communications, 1989. The authors have compiled a reference handbook of common scams, including not only classic ones, but new modifications of age-old con games that developed as fraud artists brought them into the 20th century. The book also touches upon subtle cons, such as flying saucer hoaxes designed to get your attention, waste your time, and perhaps glean fees and notoriety from the media. Written in a simple conversational style, this handbook is valuable for cop and citizen alike.

The Doctor Business, Richard Carter, NY, Pocket Books, 1967. This book, a revision of a work first published in 1958, is dated, but it's still accurate in principle. "Different names, but the same old shit." At that time, the American Medical Association was fighting to maintain the right of doctors to charge whatever they wished for services. Part of this was avoiding any sort of public control over the way doctors do business. Nothing has changed.

YOU WILL ALSO WANT TO READ: